WINNING WAYS

WINNING WAYS

LESSONS
FOR
JUNIORS
FROM THE
TOP TRAINERS

MARGARET J. CANNELL

HOWELL BOOK HOUSE
NEW YORK
•
MAXWELL MACMILLAN CANADA
TORONTO
•
MAXWELL MACMILLAN INTERNATIONAL
NEW YORK   OXFORD   SINGAPORE   SYDNEY

Howell Book House
Macmillan Publishing Company
866 Third Avenue
New York, NY 10022

Maxwell Macmillan Canada, Inc.
1200 Eglinton Avenue East
Suite 200
Don Mills, Ontario M3C 3N1

Macmillan Publishing Company is part of the Maxwell Communication Group
of Companies.

Diagrams by Amy M. Adams

Book design by Liney Li

Library of Congress Cataloging-in-Publication Data
Cannell, Margaret J.
Winning ways : lessons for juniors from the top trainers /
Margaret J. Cannell.
p.   cm.
Includes index.
ISBN 0-87605-960-4
1. Horsemanship—Study and teaching.   2. Junior riders
(Horsemanship)—Training of.   I. Title.
SF310.5.C36   1994
798.2'07—dc20   93-38198   CIP

Macmillan books are available
at special discounts for bulk purchases for sales promotions, premiums,
fund-raising, or educational use. For details, contact:

Special Sales Director
Macmillan Publishing Company
866 Third Avenue
New York, NY 10022

10 9 8 7 6 5 4 3 2 1

Printed in the United States of America

To Captain John Henderson

of the British Cavalry, who hooked me into this sport.

To Cindy Ford, who kept Chipper throughout.

To Marylon and Doug Alexander

for putting me up and putting up with me.

To Dean Hamilton, who frequently risked his self-image

to clutch the manuscript from

the hungry jaws of my computer.

And of course, to my children, Kris and Heather,

whose support never fails.

CONTENTS

PREFACE

There are millions of horses, thousands of riders and hundreds of trainers. The mathematical combinations of these numbers would seem to make for a hard go of putting you on top in the horse show ring. Luckily for us, this is not so.

In the United States today we have more fine trainers than ever before who teach more students than ever before on a greater pool of horses from all over the world. We are very fortunate.

Anyone who has ridden knows that not all horses suit all riders. What makes this sport so fair to all participants is that greatness comes when the sum of the parts is greater than the whole. In other words: $1 + 1 =$ a perfect 10. It is the trainer's job to make sure that the best one is mounted on the right one and taught well.

Just as all horses do not suit all riders, so it is that all trainers do not suit all students. It is true too that just as all horses have four legs, so do all trainers have one goal. The trainers who so generously allowed me to observe and record their lessons hope to create the next great talent while teaching all students to be competitive. There is no mystery or secret to the teaching of good riding. What separates one from another is the method by which they convey the information. It is through communication, via personality, that a student finds the most suitable trainer. I believe the instructors would agree that their job is to assist a student in discovery, to draw out conclusions and behaviors rather than entering data into some type of robot. We all know that when the rider enters the ring it is up to the horse/rider combination to succeed. The trainers interviewed for this book are able to lay a strong foundation of skills and tap into the student's mind to pull from them winning behavior.

I feel a little like I fell into the cookie jar. I got to watch these top trainers teach. I was privy to their methods and saw the fruits of their labors compete. Each teacher had his or her own way of passing on time-tested knowledge, and each stamped the lessons with a very personal signature.

There has been much talk on the softness of our junior riders. Talk that they are so consumed with winning one equitation class, they never learn how to ride or be horsemen. I am cheered by the fact that the students used in this book have ambitions that go far beyond the Medal/Maclay. In filling out a qestionnaire for me, they professed hopes to be the best they can be and with luck move on to the Grand Prix ring. Not one stopped short with the hope to win the equitation finals as a goal in itself. Students gave their trainers high praise, all of them noting the enthusiasm and knowledge of their teachers. Positive attitudes obviously beget positive attitudes.

Why were these particular trainers chosen? It is not my intention to imply they are the only trainers of note in our country. They were chosen because they have long track records of success and often shape the industry as we know it. I'm sure you will agree as you look over the list of names—it is a prestigious roll call.

Not all of you will be able to train with the teachers featured in this book. Although some of you will find your way to them, others will be constrained by economics, geography or other obstacles. It's okay. There are many fine trainers throughout the country. But, if you are serious about this best of all sports, you have an obligation to learn all you can from as many sources as possible: attend and audit clinics, read—no, make that devour—books, watch videotapes, check out our magazines, observe. Always observe. It is up to the student to seek the information and to the teacher to supply it. Use every resource at hand to better yourself, but understand that reading and watching are not doing. You need always to have a professional eye on your riding, even if it can't be daily.

It has been my job to try to convey to you the lessons taught by these professionals so that you can use them to understand more about the education of horse and rider. We are bringing you practical theory of today's junior scene, not a riding lesson for you specifically. The instructor and I don't know you or your horse. These are, for the most part, intermediate or advanced lessons. It is my goal to expose you to the best in instruction offered and hope that you will use it wisely.

The two legends who open this book—George Morris and Jimmy Williams—have shaped modern equitation. Historically, this country's riding methods have been fathered by different sires. The East Coast tradition comes from the Western European school, while the West Coast is strongly influenced by Spanish and Indian riding traditions.

George Morris carries on and refines the techniques of General Harry D. Chamberlin, author of *The American Manual of Horsemanship and Horsemastership;* Vladimir S. Littauer, a developer of "forward riding"; and, more recently, Gordon Wright. The basis of the teaching comes from the cavalry and the hunt traditions. Across the continent, Jimmy Williams brings the western tradition to the sport: the riding of the Conquistadors who founded California and other western states, and the legacy of the great riding tribes of Indians, such as the Apache and the Navaho. He calls his horse sense "cowboy psychology."

What these two men have in common is a total dedication to the horse and its relationship with man. They share a lifelong commitment to improving the sport and our knowledge. Separately, they learned the lessons that horses teach. Together, they are, directly or indirectly, responsible for all the top riders in America today. As successful as they have been, they continue to learn from the animal. They are great because of their accomplishments and because of their interest in always learning more. In equine history, they will be written of as masters.

WINNING WAYS

GEORGE MORRIS

*'You can't believe in yourself if
you aren't asked anything.'*

Parker/Cammett

GEORGE MORRIS IS THE MAN. IT IS HE WHO MOLDED AND SCULPTED THE EQUITATION DIVISION INTO ITS PRESENT FORM. HIS LIST OF CREDENTIALS IS AWE INSPIRING, BEGINNING WITH THE RECORD HE STILL HOLDS AS THE YOUNGEST WINNER OF THE MEDAL/MACLAY FINALS AT THE AGE OF FOURTEEN, UP TO AND INCLUDING PARTICIPATION ON MORE THAN ONE OLYMPIC TEAM. THERE IS NOTHING THIS MAN HAS NOT DONE IN THE FIELD OF HUNTER/JUMPERS. VIRTUALLY EVERY TEACHER IN THIS BOOK QUICKLY ACKNOWLEDGES THEIR DEBT TO GEORGE AND THE SYSTEM HE HELPED CREATE. HE HAS CREATED MANY PROFESSIONAL RIDERS AND HAS COACHED THEM ALL. AS ONE OF OUR MOST PRESTIGIOUS JUDGES, A TOP AHSA OFFICIAL, AN AUTHOR, A TEAM COACH, A BUSY CLINICIAN, HE IS STILL ONE OF THE VERY BEST TEACHERS ON THE SCENE TODAY, WITH HIS FINGERS ON THE PULSE OF THE BUSINESS. HE COULD REST ON HIS REPUTATION, BUT HE NEVER SLACKS OFF. GEORGE IS CONSTANTLY TEACHING STUDENTS FROM ALL OVER THE WORLD. HE IS GENEROUS WITH HIS KNOWLEDGE, ALWAYS READY TO SHARE IT WITH THOSE AROUND HIM.

The Flat

George is known to be a challenging teacher. He presses his students to perform above their perceived level of ability. There are no excuses in front of George, and nothing less than your very best is accepted. George's students have come to him to be pressed hard. He gives no less than he demands. He teaches constantly: in a lesson, in a warmup ring or at the ingate. He is in uniform, as always. A touch of time past, when trainers donned boots and breeches to set an example. He expects his riders to be in uniform too; it is all part of the discipline, part of the show. As he will tell you, "show" is the operative word in "horse show."

This day he's teaching in gray breeches, polished black boots, a fitted golf shirt neatly tucked in. His carefully modulated voice is theater. Without being loud, it carries a great distance. Each word in enunciated to the extreme. This is useful to the many spectators at every lesson he teaches. There is never a doubt about what he says. When George Morris speaks, everyone listens.

"Say, girls, take your feet out" is the first command to his students for this hour. "Flex your horse a little left, keep pressing until he gives to the left rein. Now change the bend to the right using your right hand, direct rein. Close your leg to push him up to the bit." George, left hand resting on his hip, waves his right arm, pushing his words out on the circle. "Now bend left again, keeping his [the horse's] body forward and straight." The students go through the alternating bending exercise under his watchful eye, "bending to the resistance, always watching with your inside leg."

George pronounces *leg* as two syllables in his special elocution that others copy, just as they adopt his methods. The students are allowed to pick up their irons and are cautioned to control pace and rhythm at the posting trot as they change direction frequently to gain submission and flexibility on both sides of the horse.

They are instructed to increase the pace of the trot without losing roundness. "If he fights with you, close your fingers to meet the resistance." George counsels "relentless patience" to a rider whose horse resists compliance.

The next warmup exercise consists of several walk-halt transitions. "Be stronger with your hands and legs until he gives," George instructs as one horse insists on throwing his head up during the halts. "Always have your horse in front of your legs and a little behind your hands . . . he should be giving. If he stiffens on the right side, bend him that way. If he stiffens on the left side, bend him that way."

Among the jumps set out in the field are several cavalletti, which George makes use of during the flat work.

He asks the students to trot a figure eight over two ground poles that are placed parallel to each other several feet apart. The students are then directed to trot the two rails as a line, getting nine trotting steps between them. He adds this to the transition exercises of trot-halt. "Don't let him back. Do it again if he backs up. In the halt be soft and supple . . . don't lower your hands—close them. Make him walk forward after a backwards step."

The students are asked for a broken line, which George explains looks like a shallow serpentine. Think of the track as looking like the outline of a peanut. "Three or four steps left, change bend and your diagonal, three or four steps right." One student is confused by the new shape and asks her horse to move away from her leg in the exercise. "No, no, no. Change your diagonal at the point of the turn. It is *not* a leg yield." George's relentless patience applies to horses. From riders he expects a mistake not be made more than once.

The riders go back to the circle figure on command. "Now go straight again, lengthen stride with care. Shorten the stride and then lengthen again with care. Let the horse die when you shorten. Lengthen again, changing direction through the diagonal—lengthening through the diagonal. Shorten the stride and sit the trot."

One of the great lessons I learned from George many years ago concerned the working area used for lessons or free work. In one of his big fields at his home farm in Hunterdon, George told me he did not fence the area because he liked to have the students imagine different work areas and then stick to them. He would ask them to ride a rectangular ring one day, a round ring the next. There was no shape he would not ask them to envision and ride, all the while incorporating exercises within the chosen shape. This is a good exercise for horse and rider discipline. There is no rail for horse or rider to depend on.

This day, George has his students working in a circle. "The shoulder-out . . . bend him around your outside rein and leg. Change to the haunches-out now. Bending him with the outside rein and pushing with your inside leg. Now to the shoulder-in, followed by the haunches-out. Go straight, lengthen his stride and change direction through the diagonal." This brings the students into a left-handed circle at the sitting trot.

"Shoulder-out with right rein and right leg. To the haunches-in . . . your left leg should be a hand behind the girth . . . to the shoulder-out." Hawklike, George watches every step without missing a detail. There are some who have ridden a lesson who swear he has eyes in the back of his head. "To the haunches-in and from the haunches-in, pick up the counter canter. Stay in the counter canter until he accepts and relaxes. If he resists on one side, bend him that way. If he gets too strong, use your half-halts to slow him down and hold him with your seat. No matter what he does with his mouth, keep the contact.

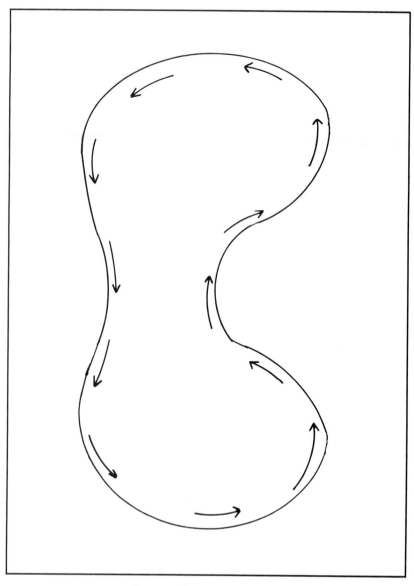

Pattern for Broken Line:
Keeping the right lead while tracking left on the pattern

Go through the diagonal and stay on the right lead." This puts the riders on a left track carrying the right, or counter, lead.

"Now girls, a broken line keeping the right lead." This is a challenging test of coordinating aids and cooperating horses. To make it clearer, visualize yourself cantering on the right lead while circling left in the peanut-shaped pattern, never letting your horse swap leads. "Keep the horse bent towards the leading leg all the time. Extend the canter gradually and carefully from your leg. Then shorten . . . sit heavier and ask him to come back . . . lengthen carefully again . . . sit heavier and shorten the canter." This is repeated until each horse is accepting of holding the lead despite the track.

After a walk break for both horse and rider, George returns to the cavalletti on the ground, asking his students to canter the poles in a straight line, getting four canter steps between them. They are working on a right-handed circle, and with each pass over the cavalletti he rolls one pole toward the other making the distance shorter and shorter. "Find the short stride. Coordinate your aids using hands, legs, seat to fit in the four." It takes a few minutes for all the riders to master the art of shortening while maintaining rhythm.

Jumping

The jumping starts after each rider has shortened her irons. It begins with a jumping-out-of-hand exercise. It is a constant turning test that requires a shortened canter stride and turning in the air.

The riders start on the right lead, canter over a rail and roll back on a small jump. "Don't let it get more and more rapid . . . stay low in the saddle and relaxed." They are instructed to reverse direction and do the exercise off the other lead. George reminds the riders they should always school off both leads. "Watch the pole in a relaxed way . . . it is a waiting game, this exercise. If he [the horse] is getting strong, just as you are landing, take his mouth a little bit." Soon the horses have softened and given to both sides. The success leads to the next exercise, which works on compression and expansion.

The riders are to canter forward to the pole (away from the barn) and on a long, open stride get down to the oxer. After the oxer they are to execute a half-turn in reverse back to the oxer, shortening the horse's stride as he heads towards the pole. "Your horse should be an

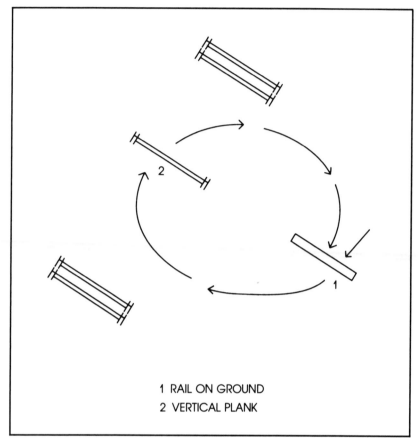

1 RAIL ON GROUND
2 VERTICAL PLANK

Turning Exercise

accordion—opening and closing and always changing. Girls, after the cavalletti, stop on the line and back up a couple steps." George doesn't give the riders a set of number of strides to ride between the jumps, allowing them to figure out a distance off the pace they carry. They will discover they need a forward pace going out and a very collected pace headed toward the barn.

The next exercise continues the accordion theme. The riders are to ride a diagonal line that is a forward three to a forward five strides.

"Get your pace before the first jump. Don't try to find a distance, just ride forward. If you do your homework in the turn, it will be easy." The jumps are raised two holes (to about 3'3") and the riders asked to get the forward three to a steady six strides, which will mean more collection to add the stride. "Line it up [the second and third jumps]

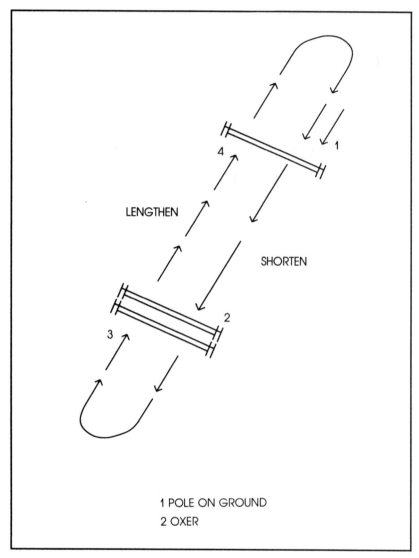

LENGTHEN

SHORTEN

1 POLE ON GROUND
2 OXER

An exercise to practice lengthening and shortening

center to left to fit the six in." The swedish oxer is raised four holes at all cups. The riders are asked to come back in the three to the five strides. "Line it up center to right to right," George advises. The oxer is adjusted again so that it is four holes higher on the right and four holes lower on the left, front and back. The riders are to get the six strides again. "Put a good bend in the six strides this time so that you jump the oxer low side to low side. This is precision riding."

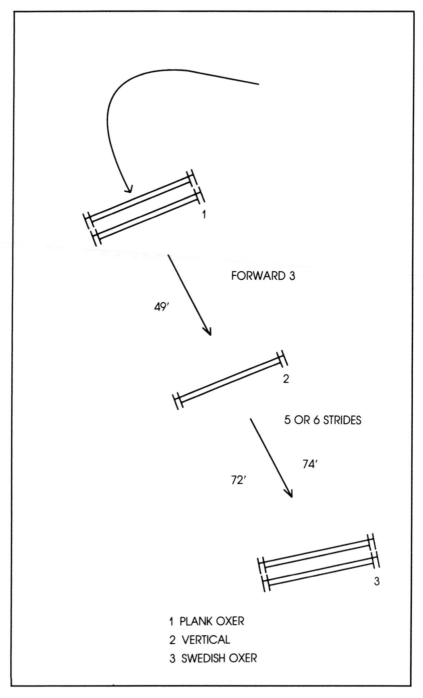

FORWARD 3

49'

2

5 OR 6 STRIDES

74'

72'

3

1 PLANK OXER
2 VERTICAL
3 SWEDISH OXER

Precision Exercise:
Riding to a specific place on the jump

The next exercise goes back to reminding the horse that he can turn and go forward at the same time. The riders are told to angle the first jump, turn in the air over the second obstacle and then gallop on to the third jump, which is a bigger square oxer. "Jump the left corner of the first jump and turn in the air. Keep your outside leg to hold the line and keep going . . . *Gallop!*" One of the horses takes exception to the rider's leg and bucks out at its pressure. "Correct that by galloping him with leg, up and down the field until he accepts your leg."

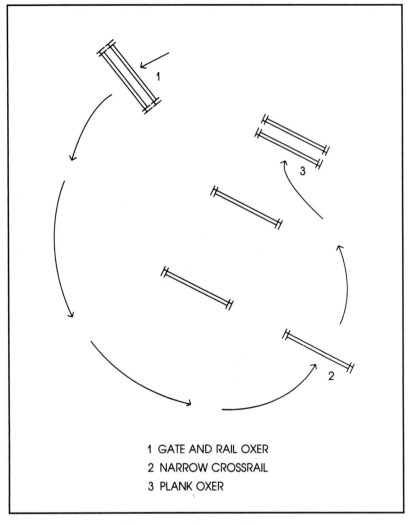

1 GATE AND RAIL OXER
2 NARROW CROSSRAIL
3 PLANK OXER

Turning Exercise with pace:
To be performed at the gallop

George is just warming up. The riders are prepared for a harder exercise ahead with directions to ride a one stride, which is a little long, to a two stride that is equally tight. The first two jumps were half-width walls; the last, a square oxer on the downhill. "Be definite in your line and distance," George warns. No sooner are the horses and riders comfortable with the combination, when George raises the stakes. The riders now have to add a jump on a difficult angle to the combination. Not only is he asking them to deal with related distances and get the line in a prescribed number of strides, but they also must find a track that will make it work. To force the riders into the hardest option, a very shallow line, George positions himself where he wants them to turn. The nature of the requested track means the in and out won't line up easily. With George physically blocking the easier track, there is no question they will have to try what he wants. He calls for seven strides to the combination. To do the numbers, they will need to carry a forward pace. Two of the students have some trouble here. They are slightly intimidated by the difficulty of the track and underride. Their horses stop the first time. One of the riders has come to the lesson without a stick. "Always with a jumper, carry a stick! Correct and come back immediately." George is firm that when a horse is disobedient, he be forced to confront the issue again quickly, not after a leisurely canter around the field. He asks his horses to concentrate as hard as his riders and his successes prove the validity of his system. The riders feel a mixture of relief and self-satisfaction at the completion of this test. Their relief is premature, they aren't finished yet. Making it even tougher, George raises the stakes and the jumps. The first jump is slanted steeply so the high side is on the side they need to jump in order to make the line George wants. The oxer is also raised. But it doesn't end there. "Girls, I want you to get six strides to the one to the two. You must make one line, you must have pace and you must be definite. You'll have to stay with the right rein over the in."

By taking a stride out of the line, one rider figures she'll have to fly to get to the combination. She gets there disorganized and pulls up. Striding toward her, a scowl on his face, George chastises her. "You are not strong enough mentally . . . this is riding." With the added push, she is able to ride the exercise successfully.

As a finale to the lesson, George asks the riders to pick up a gallop and go to a large gray wall standing at about 4 feet 9 inches. The wall, solid and flanked by two gigantic standards, looks like a building. A

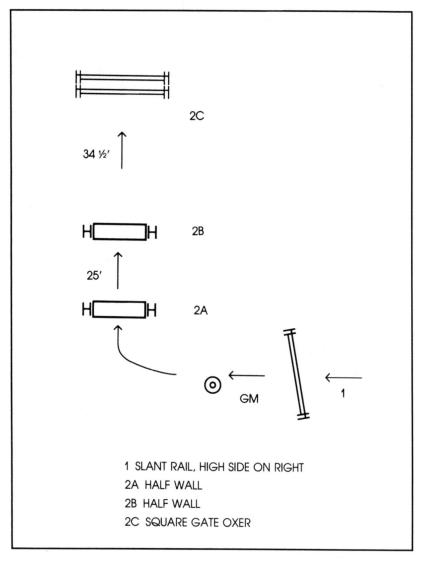

2C

34 ½'

2B

25'

2A

GM

1

1 SLANT RAIL, HIGH SIDE ON RIGHT
2A HALF WALL
2B HALF WALL
2C SQUARE GATE OXER

Making a shallow speed track:
Finding the fastest track
through direction rather than speed

very tall building. The riders, one by one, start to canter down to the jump. When they are three strides away, George calls out, "Drop your stirrups before the jump and pick them up on the other side . . . and gallop!" Eyes wide, each rider jumps the wall twice without stirrups before being told to ride in.

The riders stand before George, pleased with themselves. They only tackled the difficulties because George told them to. In their heart of hearts, they weren't always sure they were up to his demands. "You can't believe in yourself if you are not asked anything," George tells them. "Don't be perfect over three-foot jumps, that doesn't prove anything. You'll get more confidence testing yourselves. I know you can do more that you think you can."

Step by step this lesson tested the students who participated. They were all on good, made horses, which enabled George to push them. Step by step he led them into challenging exercises.

George has been one of the voices decrying the state of our junior riders. He judges and trains extensively, and what he's seeing is disturbing to him. For all junior riders in this country, there are only a few who measure up to international standards.

The lack of depth can be blamed on many things. Few dispute that one area of concern is the number and type of horse shows. In order to accommodate a large number of entries within a specific time frame and for profit purposes, the majority of the courses are not challenging to riders. Sadly, too few juniors see a course that isn't very easy and quite low. It is George's belief that the repetition of these easy courses has taught our juniors to master only the simplest of skills. In the name of winning, they do not take on the uncomfortable challenges that encourage growth. Regardless of the students' level of mastery, George can challenge them to be better riders. They are shown that they can do more than just pose over a side, diagonal, side course.

❏ *Information on clinics or lessons with George Morris can be obtained by contacting Hunterdon, R.D.#1, Box 319, Pittstown, NJ 08867; 908-782-0126.*

JIMMY WILLIAMS

Bronson Photography

"Luck is as good as brains as long as it lasts."

THE VERY FIRST TIME THE AHSA CHOSE TO PRESENT A LIFETIME ACHIEVEMENT AWARD IT WAS GIVEN TO JIMMY WILLIAMS. THAT HONOR OCCURRED IN 1991 AND WAS ONE OF MANY HE RECEIVED. JIMMY WAS ALSO HONORED IN HIS LIFETIME WITH INDUCTION INTO THE EQUESTRIAN HALL OF FAME AND AS AHSA HORSEMAN OF THE YEAR. THE FAMED HORSEMAN WHO DRESSED TO THE TWO INFLUENCES IN HIS LIFE—A COWBOY HAT ABOVE BOOTS AND BREECHES—DIED IN THE FALL OF 1993, SOON AFTER THE RESEARCH FOR THIS BOOK WAS COMPLETED. ALTHOUGH WE ARE ALL POORER FOR HIS DEATH, I HAVE DECIDED TO LEAVE THE CHAPTER IN THE PRESENT TENSE, AS HIS SYSTEM IS STILL ALIVE THROUGH THE TEACHING OF THE MANY PROFESSIONAL RIDERS TRAINED IN THE WILLIAMS METHOD.

JIMMY, SON OF A HORSE TRADER, BEGAN AS A WESTERN TRAINER AND DID STUNT WORK IN THE MOVIES. HE RECEIVED A PATSY AWARD FOR HIS TRAINING OF THE EQUINE STAR IN *THE HORSE IN THE GRAY FLANNEL SUIT*. JIMMY ALWAYS HAD A SPECIAL RELATIONSHIP WITH HORSES. PEOPLE WHO HAVE WORKED WITH HIM SAY HE COULD POSITIVELY SEE INTO A HORSE'S MIND. HE CALLED THAT "COWBOY PSYCHOLOGY." IT WAS 1959 WHEN JIMMY CHANGED HIS FOCUS TO THE HUNTER/JUMPER RING AND BEGAN TURNING OUT WINNING RIDERS AND HORSES. BETWEEN THAT TIME AND 1993, HE WAS RESPONSIBLE FOR TURNING OUT HUNDREDS OF TOP HORSES AND AS MANY AS FORTY TOP PROFESSIONALS. JIMMY TOLD ME THAT TOO MANY TRAINERS TODAY ARE TURNING OUT RING RIDERS RATHER THAN FUTURE PROFESSIONALS. HE HAS TRAINED A HALF-DOZEN OLYMPIC TEAM RIDERS, INCLUDING ANNE KURSINSKI, HAP HANSEN, MARY CHAPOT AND ROBERT RIDLAND.

SUSIE HUTCHISON, HIS CO-TRAINER IN THE LAST YEARS, HAS AN ENVIABLE LIST OF CREDITS HERSELF. SHE HAS SPENT HER YEARS LEARNING THE PARTICULAR WISDOM THAT WAS JIMMY WILLIAMS' AND SHE HAS DONE WELL. SHE HAS RIDDEN ON OUR NATION'S CUP TEAM, COMPETED IN MANY WORLD CUP COMPETITIONS AND HAS BEEN AWARDED THE TOP HONOR IN THE MERCEDES CHALLENGE SERIES. SHE IS CONSISTENTLY IN THE GRAND PRIX RIBBONS ON BOTH COASTS AND STILL HAS MANY MORE VICTORIES AHEAD.

The Flat

"**P**retty is as pretty does" sums up his attitude toward riding. "If the horse is happy, and doing what you want, you are doing your job." The stiff, overarched rider looking for a mirror is not the student he produces. He produces riders, and more importantly to him, future trainers. Jimmy is a translator for horse and human. Communication with both is his goal. He works at teaching each to read and understand the other. While I was not able to watch a Jimmy Williams lesson in person, I was able to extensively interview Susie on the Williams program for developing riders. It is that general program that I pass along to you.

Jimmy has many "phases" he uses to create riders. One of the first things he wants a rider to understand is seat. "Seat is a mediator. Seat is complimentary to hand and to leg." In further explanation, Jimmy says that seat and leg together teach a horse to go forward or gain impulsion, while seat and hand teach a horse to come back, or collect. One of the exercises he uses to teach the novice student about seat is to have the rider sit on her hands, palms side up. The rider is asked to sit on the seat bones as in a normal walk position. Feeling the contact with the seat bones, the rider is then asked to sit in front of her seat bones, by closing her hip angle and moving toward the half-seat position. As soon as the position is attained, the rider can feel that her seat bones are no longer in her palms. Finally, the rider is asked to sit behind her seat bones, a deep position used to push a horse forward. All of these are first done at the standstill so riders can be aware of the different feel of each use of their seat.

Jimmy uses the lunge line lesson to continue teaching his belief that leg and seat are the most important aids a rider can master. He gives the rider no reins, forcing the student to learn to control pace and direction from the options left: seat and leg. Additionally, he wants the rider to blend and become a part of the horse. As students move up in strength, they will be lunged without reins and asked to post and half-seat the trot and canter gaits without the benefit of their irons.

When teaching, Jimmy is trying to "get into the subconscious mind of the rider." He peppers his explanations with concepts geared to the age of the student. If it is an adult rider, he will use metaphors that adults understand without thought, such as driving a car. If it is a child rider, the explanations talk to the childhood experience, such as riding a bicycle. He even has a pair of handlebars he can attach to a specially rigged bridle to teach youngsters the concept of giving with one hand when taking with the other. Famous for his unique methods of communicating to riders, Jimmy's goal is always to find things that are familiar to riders so they are able to carry knowledge they already have into the new sport of riding. He will tell you that in order for students to remember, the experience must be personal. He explains how making an experience personal leaves a lasting impression. "If I went to a party and met fifty people, how many would remember my name? If I decide I want to get the attention of a certain person, I might, perhaps, spill a drink on her. You can bet she'll remember my name as I apologize. In fact, she won't forget that for a very long time!" Keeping it personal is very much what Jimmy's method is about.

"With most riders, you only get into their conscious minds. It's in one ear and out the other. When they ride out of the ring it's over. I'm always telling them not to ride around the ring with their brains in neutral." To Jimmy, the challenge of getting into a rider's mind and making it easy to learn is paramount.

Jimmy does a lot of work on teaching riders about pace. He tells them that if they cover 360 yards in a minute with a twelve-foot stride, they are going twelve miles per hour. That is the speed at which most hunters and equitation horses are asked to perform. To help reinforce the notion of a speedometer, he has wheeled off the yardage around his ring, from the palm tree to the lamppost. The riders are then asked to canter that distance in one minute. If they get there too fast, they are over the pace. If they exceed the one-minute time allowed, they are under the required speed.

Transitions play a big role in the flat work of all students at Flintridge. Jimmy wants to make sure the riders can regulate their horses on the flat before they face the jumps. If they are unsuccessful without the jumps, they will have to rely on dumb luck when the fences are set. "Luck is as good as brains as long as it lasts" is a Jimmyism.

It is important to Jimmy that the riders do more than consider the horse as a form of transportation. He strives to have them understand the animal and wants the riders to "really listen to the horse." He tells the rider to watch the inside ear of the horse as a signal the horse is listening to what is being asked. "Draw the horse to your inside leg. Converse with your horse. His inside ear should be back, listening to your leg. If his inside ear goes forward, you have lost his attention and you'll have to draw him back again from your leg." Jimmy says that the inside ear should be back during all flat work, even the flat work on course. The outside ear can move back and forth, but the inside ear tells the rider if the horse is paying attention.

Another favorite Jimmy exercise is posting at the canter, which he calls "the one-two." This is a suppling exercise for the rider and at the same time is relaxing for the horse. The rider half-seats on "one" and sits on "two." The rhythm is one-two, one-two, one-two. The purpose of this exercise is to teach riders the job of seat and the influence of weight. They learn to be able to change the seat without use of the hands for balance, and to change stride without clutching.

All of the exercises Jimmy teaches are aimed truly at rider effectiveness. None are specifically designed to make a pretty-looking rider, although it's not surprising that a confident rider draws an attractive picture.

Jumping

The jumping chute is well used in the Williams method. In the chute, seven bounces are set at a low height. It is a very controlled environment, where the horse has little choice but to jump the line of bounces and then stop, reverse and go back through them. The jumps are 18 inches high, set 12 feet apart so that the speed at which the horse will be going is the optimum twelve miles per hour. The chute is a place for riders to learn about body balance and pace. Often, Jimmy not only takes the reins away, but also the entire bridle, so the rider has to control the horse through leg and seat. He says he uses the exceptionally well trained horse for this exercise: the horse who is well schooled and relaxed in the chute experience. Without the reins, the rider has a series of arm swings and positions to work out over the jumps. With some riders, a blindfold is produced and tied over their eyes before they continue the exercise. The object is to teach the rider independence in the air, balance, and to be one with the horse over the jumping effort.

Tish Quirk

Susie Hutchison aboard Samsung Woodstock

Jimmy uses a variety of other gymnastic exercises outside the chute in his training program. It is important that the jumps be set on the twelve-foot stride to teach pace, but he warns, "Watch for boredom" from the horse, and vary the routine to prevent it.

He has designed many exercises to deal with rider problems. He points out that riders who jump ahead of the motion usually do so because they are riding below the pace. The correction is one of his many pace exercises. Riders who stand up at the jumps usually do so because they are bracing off the stirrup too much. He'll take the stirrups away to correct this fault. A rider who opens too early in the air? If all

17

else fails he will get out the "indicator," which is a special rig he has designed that is worn by the rider. It makes a real impression if the rider snaps back in the air. "It is a very personal way for a rider to remember and feel. It helps conquer mistakes." Despite his use of specially designed contraptions for both horse and rider, he is a believer in the snaffle bit and slow learning, saying in an ideal world "There is no substitute for time." But he is a realist too. Time is not what it used to be, with the show season extended to eleven months of every year. He has found that somtimes a stressful situation will help a horse or a rider work through a problem more quickly.

It is one of Jimmy's goals that the riders and horses be able to teach themselves. By making skills easy for them, they learn to do the right thing from the beginning. This is the reason behind his use of cones and flags. He might place cones in the corners of the ring so the riders always learn to steer deep around the turns. He will put cones or flags on the landing side of jumps to create good habits or to cure bad ones. Two flags placed 5 feet apart centered on the landing side will force the rider to find the center of the jump and keep true to the track through the air. A rider with an overpowering left hand may find a flag placed in the center of the jump, with the instruction he must jump the right side. Riders learning to angle jumps may find flags on the landing side, directing them to the correct path. After they perform the exercise correctly, the flags will be removed and the rider will naturally follow the same path. Jimmy says he puts the markers behind the jumps so that a rider is always monitoring the horse's path in flight. No resting on the neck, no crest release, no allowing the horse to drift one direction or the other. Riders are to be able to make the necessary adjustments to get the required results.

Counting is an exercise used to teach depth perception and speed recognition. He will have a rider count aloud one stride from the fence. Then two strides away. One, two, three strides to the jump and so on up to five or six strides away. "That [counting] is our only means of having a speedometer." He might then ask the rider to jump a line in striding measured for the perfect twelve mile per hour ride. He might ask the rider to move up the pace to a speed of fourteen miles per hour, eliminating a stride from the line. He might ask to see a ride under pace, at about ten miles per hour where the rider should add an extra stride between the two jumps. He will work with his students on this exercise to make them more aware of the pace they are carrying.

Jimmy's "cowboy psychology" is at work here too. "The horse's ear is a good indication of what is going on in his mind during jumping. Thirty feet before the jump, both ears should come forward. That shows he is checking his depth perception, ready to jump. If he cocks an ear back, he is losing attention and may well run out to that side." If the horse cocks one ear back, Jimmy advises quickly getting the horse's attention on the opposite side to the flattened ear. "If he puts his left ear back, draw him with your right leg. Then use both legs."

Jimmy doesn't believe in the crest release and works at getting his riders to be so secure in their seat that they can maintain a light contact with the horse's mouth. He doesn't want to see a horse being grabbed in the mouth, nor does he want to see a rider throw the mouth away.

Rick Osteen

Susie Hutchison on High Heels concentrates on the next obstacle.

"There should be no slack in the reins. The hand should be following the motion of the horse's neck."

One turning exercise used is a line of jumps basically alongside of each other across the width of the ring. Here, Jimmy works on teaching the students to turn accurately. "You'll make better time with careful tight turns than you will with speed. If you get going too fast, you'll slide by the jumps." He will have students work on this exercise until the length of the turn is reduced drastically. And he'll watch the horse's ears to make sure the horse and rider are "conversing."

Natural obstacles are introduced either to riders on experienced horses or with an experienced horse in the lead. Flintridge has many natural jumps of various heights, so the junior can learn on small banks and the like before moving on to the tougher obstacles. It is approached as a fun thing to do. Co-instructor and Grand Prix rider Susie Hutchison says, "If you tell kids that it's hard, they'll worry." Jimmy does want the kids to have fun and he makes sure that they do. Flintridge juniors are encouraged to be a team even in competition. The top juniors ride several horses a day and take three to four lessons a week. The students are encouraged to give their input. They critique each other and praise each other. The goal is to learn to ride rather than to learn to beat someone. Susie believes that "riding is a mental sport. It all comes down to who concentrated hardest on any given day." When one Flintridge rider wins, all are successful. Jimmy says there are a lot of good riders in this country, but not many good trainers.

He's doing more than his share to add to our bank of future trainers.

❏ *Clinic information for Susie Hutchison can be obtained by contacting Flintridge Riding Club, 4625 Oak Grove Drive, Flintridge, CA 91001; 818-952-1233.*

MISSY CLARK

"Without proper basics, all other aspects can't be attained."

Cannell

FOR TEN YEARS MISSY CLARK, IN PARTNERSHIP WITH GEOFF TEALL AND RANDY ROY, HAS WORKED AT PRODUCING WINNERS AT THEIR NORTH RUN FACILITY IN EAST AURORA, NEW YORK. ONE OF THEIR BEST YEARS TO DATE MUST HAVE BEEN 1991, WHEN RIDER LAURA BOWDEN WON THE AHSA MEDAL AND PLACED SECOND IN THE USET FINALS. TEAMMATE STACY BROWN PLACED FOURTH IN THE ASPCA MACLAY THE SAME YEAR. SUCCESSFUL JUNIOR SHEILA BURKE HAS ALSO PLACED IN THE EQUITATION FINALS AND HAS NOW MOVED UP TO THE GRAND PRIX RING ABOARD TARCO. NORTH RUN HUNTERS WIN BIG TOO. IN 1990, ENGINEER BROUGHT HOME THE GREEN CONFORMATION TRI-COLOR FROM HARRISBURG. IN 1992 NEWMARKET WAS AWARDED THE TITLE OF WINTER EQUESTRIAL FESTIVAL LARGE JUNIOR HUNTER CHAMPION. THESE ARE JUST TWO OF MANY OTHER HUNTERS WHO HAVE WON PRESTIGIOUS HONORS OVER THE YEARS. GEOFF TEALL CREDITS HIS ASSOCIATES MISSY CLARK AND KIP ROSENTHAL WITH THE SUCCESS OF THE JUNIORS THEY CO-TRAIN, SAYING, RATHER MODESTLY, THEY DO ALL THE WORK.

The Flat

"The winners of today's junior classes are those riders who are schooled thoroughly in the basics, are mounted properly, have worked their way up the ranks through their respective divisions and have competed at many top-level horse shows where the competition is the toughest."

With that statement, Missy admits she is a "fanatic about teaching basics. Without proper basics, all other aspects can't be attained." She also tells me that she is constantly reviewing a rider's position, regardless of their level of expertise. When schooling riders, she likes to break courses down into parts or sections. "I break down certain parts of a show ring ride into a series of 'rules.' The 'rules' may be modified but they do not vary. Each lesson is a practice session of one or more of these 'riding rules.' Over time, these fundamentals become instinctive for the riders, which allows them to be freed up to concentrate on other questions the course may pose." Missy says she likes to educate her students in as many areas as possible on the flat. She teaches lengthenings and shortenings, simple transitions, flexion, impulsion and various dressage movements. "I want my riders to understand how important flat work is in the whole process of riding. Without correct flat work and preparation, it is almost impossible to be successful today."

An example of her flat work is demonstrated by two advanced equitation riders. "Even when they are advanced," she reminds me, "I am constantly monitoring their position."

The riders begin at the walk. "Work your horses forward, and out on the circle off your inside leg. Keep your eye up, watching the track you are holding your horse on, and if you feel he falls behind, you've got to work it forward before you sort out the contact. Always think forward first." Missy reminds one rider that a better use of her eye will help her sluggish horse to go forward, as will a more active seat. As the posting trot begins, Missy advises the riders to keep the track and the pace: "Get yourself on a circle that is consistent in size and shape . . . check that your posting trot is up to pace at roughly eight miles per hour. Secondly, check that your inside leg is keeping your horse out on the circle. If your horse wants to fall in on the circle you correct it with forward motion and inside leg keeping him out." As the students gain willingness from their horses, they are encouraged to reward the animals. "When you feel that he makes that adjustment out . . . that his shoulders move out . . . you can reward him with a give on the inside rein." As the trot gains thrust, Missy offers a position check. "A little lower and lighter with your posting . . . watch you don't allow your seat to get too high."

The riders are asked for a sitting trot at about six miles per hour. "As you fall back in speed, watch that you don't allow the trot to become dead. You need to keep his back legs propelling you forward so that it's collected but a little lively at the same time. Concentrate on feeling his back legs.

"On the circle, I want to see you bring your horse to a shoulder-in and then straighten again, showing a little lengthening of stride after the shoulder-in. As you sit the trot, ride it forward to about eight miles per hour, lengthening his stride, and when you finish the corner, collect your horse again, showing me another shoulder-in." Missy is in constant physical motion during her lessons, humming with intensity as she rides each horse herself inside her mind. "After the next corner, lengthen your horse again down the other side and repeat the shoulder-in when you get in front of me." As the riders work on the elasticity of their animals, Missy's watchful eye keeps a check of the rider's form, offering reminders and corrections to make the work easier and smoother.

"Now, instead of the shoulder-in on this side, I want to see the shoulder out on the next pass . . . making sure that your horse doesn't fall behind your leg when you ask him for the shoulder-out. I want to see more of a lengthening down the other side too, remembering to go forward first before anything else." The rider uses her stick to encourage respect for her leg. "That was smart to use your stick. If you find he is ignoring your leg, that is the right thing to do. If he happens to break into the canter when you ask for more, canter forward a little bit before you adjust back to the trot, because in essence his response is a backwards one. The canter step is a message he is falling behind your leg." Missy asks the riders to move up to the eight miles per hour trot and execute a turn on the haunch to the left. "Keep your horse bent in the direction of movement as you begin changing track with your turn on the haunch." The students are told to post the trot. "Be fussy about riding the sit trot out, riding it out until you feel that your six miles per hour hits eight miles per hour before you start to post. That is the correct upward transition from your sit trot to your posting trot." The riders are asked to show a lengthening of stride to a strong trot. Missy often counsels her riders to "be fussy" about monitoring the horse. It is advice she adheres to in her riding and her teaching.

Back at the sitting trot, the riders are told to drop their irons and show the shoulder-in again. "Watch that he doesn't fall behind. Keep track of his haunch with your right leg. Keep his haunch on the track as you bring his shoulder in with your right rein. Missy then adds to

Kym Ketcham

*Jackie Nugent demonstrating bend in the
direction of movement*

the exercise with her students working a rectangle around her. "Then straighten him; go to the posting trot without your stirrups down the back side and repeat the exercise of collecting him on this side, showing a shoulder out this time." The riders are reminded to find a focal point ahead so they don't lose the track they want to keep the horse on. The exercise is repeated once more.

"This time after lengthening on the far side, collect again in the corner. At the midpoint of this side, just in front of me, I want you to step into the canter. Your horse's neck position should be slightly right. When you go down the back side, I want to see a lengthening of his canter before you collect him again."

After shortening and lengthening a couple of times, the riders are asked to show a simple change to the counter canter through the walk. "Take the time to be fussy about positioning your horse's neck, working him off your inside leg." The riders are then asked to straighten the horse's neck in front of Missy and show a flying change to the correct lead, followed by a lengthening of stride with a soft contact to the mouth. "You are still maintaining smooth contact, keeping that shape through his neck, but watch that your hands don't become too heavy and prevent him from going forward." A collected canter is asked for and the riders are told to pick up their stirrups as they are cantering. "Draw your toe up first to find the stirrup." As soon as the irons are recovered, the riders are instructed to change direction through a half-turn, keeping the right lead as they track left. "Take the time to shift his haunch out to keep the counter lead, keeping your hip angle open."

Missy asks the riders to come up the quarter line on the other side of the figure and show a few strides of the half-pass to the right at the canter. "Try to give a little when you can, on the right rein. Watch your turn isn't too sharp." The riders repeat the exercise: lengthening the canter on the far side, collecting in the turn and showing the half-pass to the right on the near side. "Make sure your horse is bent in the direction of movement. Keep his shoulders and haunch on one line." After reversing, the riders are told to half-seat at a hand gallop to allow the horses to stretch out and relax. "Don't let your contact [with the mouth] change drastically when you shift into your half-seat.

"Sit the saddle first, then make another downward transition to the sitting trot. You need to drop your heel as you make the downward transition and open your [hip] angle a little bit." Another reverse turn and change of direction at the sit trot follows.

To finish, Missy has the riders go back to the posting trot and tells them to allow the reins to slip through their fingers so the horse can stretch his neck out in a relaxed, low trot. "If he raises up his head and neck, ask him to stretch out again." The students reverse, allowing their horses to stretch out in the other direction also.

Jumping

We had limited jumps at our disposal, but that did not deter Missy from testing her students' ability to translate their flat work into jumping mode.

To encourage her students to be precise in the work they do, a one/two stride in and out is set up for our first exercise. Missy asks the students to angle the vertical then roll back, jumping the oxer. One rider finds trouble at the second fence. She does what many riders do when they try to force a distance; she pulls back in hopes of finding the takeoff spot. "When you're on your line to the jump, relax a little through your elbow. Give, and keep following to your jump in the same rhythm. Don't make changes. What you like to do when you're unsure is to begin slowing down, taking your rhythm away. Instead, keep the rhythm and keep following until you let the distance show itself." One of the criticisms of this generation of young riders is that they have learned to back up to find the jumps. I found that Missy and every other trainer in this book are working hard to prevent that.

Another rider finds the change difficult to accomplish after the first jump. Missy notices the rider is looking down at the landing, which allows the horse to wander off the straight and narrow. "When you are working on the angle, be fussy about your track. You are holding your horse straight to the track with two hands and finding your landing track before you ask for the change of lead. If you look down in the air, you won't even know he has left the track. Your eye plays a big part in keeping to the track."

A third rider finds trouble with the distance because she is late to recognize that her horse is slowing down to the jump. "You have a short turn and a spooky horse, you need to check your pace out of the turn and not let him fall behind."

Pace is the subject of the next exercise. Here the riders are going to have to be strong about collecting their horses and equally dedicated to moving them up. The riders are asked to canter a tall crossrail, turn left, canter a thirty-foot in-and-out fitting in two strides, and roll back on the in backwards. Then they are to trot the crossrail, and from the dead pace a trot jump creates enough motor to canter the thirty-foot combination in one long stride.

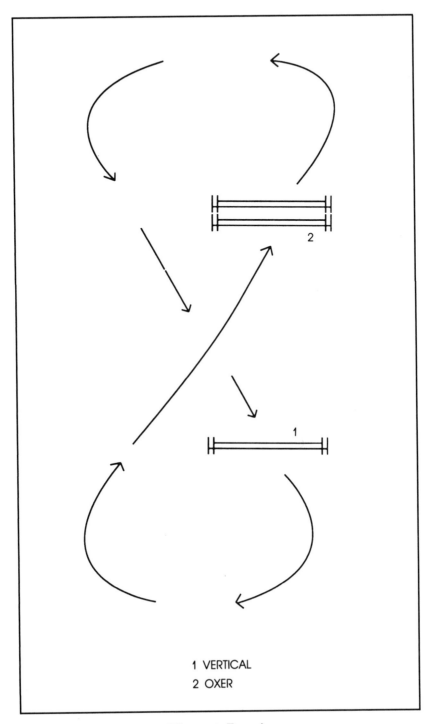

1 VERTICAL
2 OXER

Warmup Exercise

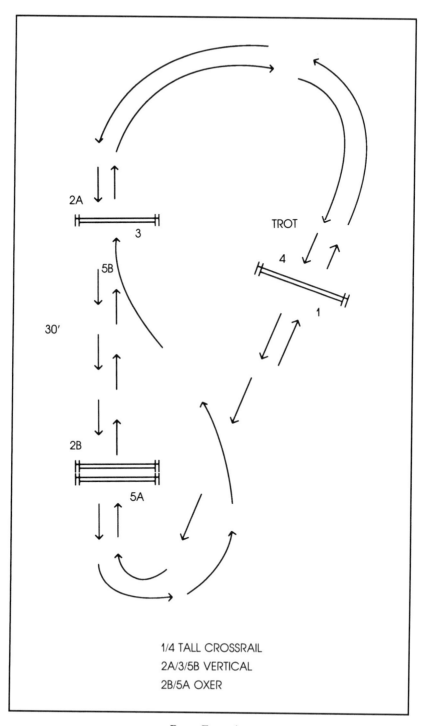

2A

3

5B

30'

TROT

4

1

2B

5A

1/4 TALL CROSSRAIL
2A/3/5B VERTICAL
2B/5A OXER

Pace Exercise

Kym Ketcham

Jackie Nugent showing a modified release

The first rider to be challenged doesn't press enough for the long one stride in and out. Her horse, who just was asked for two strides, gives it to her again. "The most important thing about riding is being able to go forward. You have to ride above the pace to get that combination in one stride and you didn't. It's a good exercise to ride above

29

pace." Riding above the pace is generally accepted as a way of teaching riders a more agile eye for distances.

Some of the riders find difficulty with the long one stride while others discover the short two stride harder for their horses. As these students watch each other, Missy is commenting on the performances. She wants her students to be able to watch competitors in the show ring and relate those trips to their own horses.

One rider is mounted on a well-broke, kind, big-strided horse. She is careful about getting to the short two stride with a collected canter, but it is still tight for him. Missy quizzes her, "What would the next step be in getting that smoothly? What else can you do besides come in on a collected stride? The rider answers correctly, that she could modify her release. "This is a sophisticated release and not one for beginner riders," Missy tells me as she instructs her student to give a short, low release that "will stall him in the air, making him jump shallow so he has more room in the distance."

Missy reminds them that they must be just as active to extend the pace as they are when they collect the pace. The riders work through the exercise until the twos and ones come easily.

The riders are given an equitation test to perform. The first test asks the riders to jump across the oxer in the in-and-out, roll back on the vertical, canter the big crossrail, walk, show a turn on the haunches to the left, counter canter back to the crossrail in the other direction and ride the in-and-out in two strides.

One rider makes the mistake of turning on the haunches to the right instead of left. "No matter how well she performs the course," Missy tells the others, "If it were a class, she'd be out. It is critical to follow directions in a test." It is a fact that many judges like to call the testing riders into the ring so they have to sort out the test without a trainers help.

Another rider hurries the turn on the haunches, losing definition of the maneuver in the process. "Don't hurry, take all the time you want. Don't let your concerns with the next part rush you through this part. Take each thing as it comes." As the riders repeat the exercise to smooth out their transitions and departs, Missy reminds them of how position can help them in the test.

The final exercise is an awareness test. The riders are to jump down a seven-stride line, turn and jump a fence placed at a right angle to

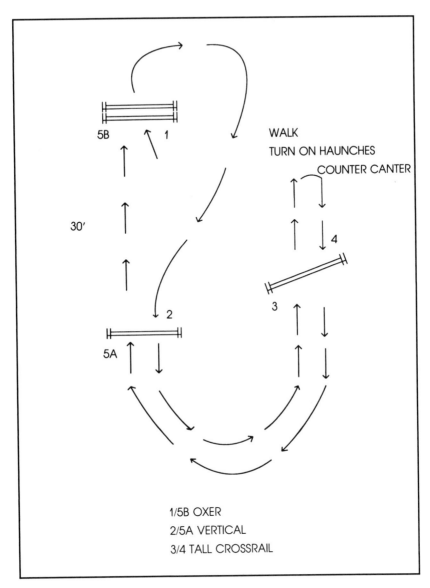

5B

1

WALK

TURN ON HAUNCHES

COUNTER CANTER

30'

4

3

2

5A

1/5B OXER

2/5A VERTICAL

3/4 TALL CROSSRAIL

Equitation Test

the line, identify which lead they have landed on and turn the opposite direction, counter cantering the line again in eight strides.

The first rider fares well until the counter canter. "You want an easy jump before the counter lead and then you want to collect him and displace his haunch—doing a haunches-out. You found a big spot

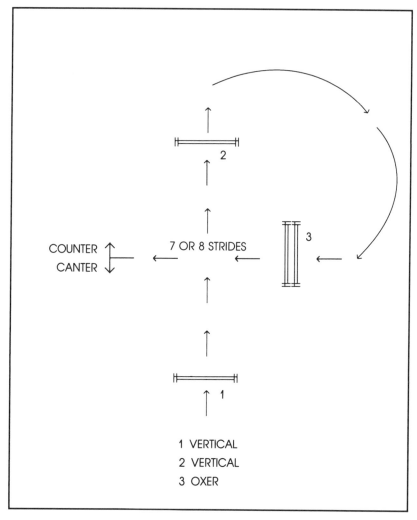

COUNTER CANTER

7 OR 8 STRIDES

2

3

1

1 VERTICAL
2 VERTICAL
3 OXER

Awareness Exercise

which carried you on landing, and then you didn't react quickly enough to hold the haunches to the counter lead." The next rider has similar problems. "The biggest fault you girls have is being late to realize what lead your horse is landing on. That makes you late in placing their haunches."

Missy reverses the exercise. Again there are problems with the counter canter. "This takes practice," Missy says as she has these riders take the course in a small bite. They will canter fence 3 and show the counter canter after the jump before doing the line. By breaking the test into segments, the riders have more time to consider the problems.

Missy admits her program isn't especially unique. Neither is basic flat work, but it still is essential to good jumping. Her style is pleasantly demanding, and she expects her students to be dedicated to learning all they can about the sport. It is not enough that they be punctual and prepared for lessons and the show ring. She encourages them to watch the great riders and learn. She nudges them to read, learn and explore.

❏ *Clinic information can be obtained by contacting Sandy Krajewski, North Run, Box 264, East Aurora, NY 14052; 716-652-6428.*

BILL COONEY

"Natural jumps make more independent riders."

Kym Ketcham

BILL COONEY AND FRANK MADDEN BEGAN THEIR PARTNERSHIP BY ASSUMING THE JUNIOR RIDERS OF GEORGE MOR-RIS'S HUNTERDON STABLES WHEN GEORGE MOVED ON TO CONQUER NEW FIELDS WITH HIS OWN RIDING. FOR MANY YEARS THEIR STUDENTS EXCELLED IN ALL THE JUNIOR DISCIPLINES. MANY WENT ON TO BECOME TOP PROFESSIONALS, IN-CLUDING PETER AND MARK LEONE, LISA TARNAPOL, CANDICE SCHLOM, MOLLY ASHE, ALICE DEBANY, SCOTT HOFFSTEADER, GARY YOUNG, JOAN SCHARFFENBERGER AND LISA JACQUIN. BILL FEELS HE HAS BEEN BLESSED BY THE HORSES THAT HAVE BEEN A PART OF HIS CAREER. DILLON, CHARGE ACCOUNT, GOZZI, MASTER DAN, PLAYING GAMES, RAIN FOREST, KAWAHMA AND MEMPHIS ARE JUST A FEW WHO EXCELLED UNDER HIS CARE. CURRENTLY, BILL IS TRAINING AT CELLULAR FARM IN CONNECTICUT. HIS PRESENT STARS INCLUDE LAUREN HOUGH AND SAMANTHA DARLING.

The Flat

Bill is a self-professed perfectionist. The details engage him. He cares, most personally, about every aspect of the showing experience from the big picture to the smallest detail. And he'll admit he is a lover of quality. As a former art student, he is by nature visual. Lines, appearances, the tiny strokes that make the whole picture are important to him. He personally supervises everything from the quality of the hay to the execution of a perfect equitation ride.

The lesson was held at Cellular Farm. If ever a facility and a person match, this is it. The farm is luxurious and immaculate. There is no clutter to distract from its simple elegance. Brass fittings on huge stalls sparkle in the sunlight. The manicured grass looks less like vegetation than a green blanket. Even the fountain bubbles modestly, as if it does not want to leave water marks on the stone pathways.

The lesson is held in a large area overlooking the surrounding county. Adorning the field are all the natural obstacles found in the big Grand Prix courses and the USET finals, in addition to the usual assortment of regular jumper fences. The students begin at the walk after a brief loosening up on their own. Ordinarily, Bill would not ask horses that are jumping to spend a great deal of time with flat work. "Ten, fifteen minutes of suppling exercises is enough if they are going to school." Make no mistake, this is a show barn, and the horses and riders are on the road almost every week of the year, from January to finals. When they are home, it is usually a rest period.

"Start with first things first. Watch that your horses are walking forward in the direction of contact, without letting them slow down when you close your fingers. Don't worry about their shape right now. Just concentrate on them walking forward and feel that the reins are starting to get a bit heavier." He uses this time to have each rider take stock of her own body position. Bill is a craftsman who stamps his riders with a quest for excellence and attention to detail.

The students go to the posting trot. "As you go forward, the horse's weight should go to the outside rein." Bill works a lot on the importance of forward motion. "Don't let the horse slow down when you take contact with your inside rein and leg. With every stride, suggest he go forward. If the horse doesn't respond to your leg, add a little spur. If he doesn't listen to your spur, just rest your stick alongside your leg for reinforcement. Concentrate on keeping your horse steady and smooth." Bill also asks the riders to monitor their rein length, saying that as the horses accept the contact and come into a frame, the students will need to check that their reins haven't become too long in view of the horse's new head and neck carriage.

After several walk-trot transitions, the riders change direction. The change creates a situation where the riders lose some of the impulsion they had gained. Bill cautions one rider, "Don't rest your hands on the withers. If your horse slows down, increase your leg and carry your hands. By now you should be able to do more and more from your leg and less and less with your reins. If the horse gets stiff to your inside rein, fix it by touching him with your inside spur. When he gives, give back." The students are asked to show the sitting trot, again thinking about continuing pace. "Put the horses around your inside rein without them slowing down. If they try to escape by wagging their heads or shifting their bodies, correct it from your leg. Touch them with the spur if needed. Don't let them get out of doing their job. You are past the point of asking them to go forward. You are now telling them to go forward."

A medium posting trot is asked for. In Bill's terminology, a medium trot is halfway between a working trot and an extended trot. "On the circle [right], I want you to change your bend and diagonal." This action places the horses on the outside bend. He explains further how the counter bend is affecting their rein aids, "Now your right rein is becoming a bearing rein." He pushes his riders to create more animation in the trot. They change back to the right bend and diagonal as Bill asks for an extended posting trot. "The more you make them go forward, the more relaxed they're going to get," The riders are asked to walk and halt, keeping the horses' attention in both downward transitions. Again, Bill uses this slow time to have the riders check their body positions. He is teaching them to monitor themselves so they can be in the most effective position to accomplish the task at hand.

Back to the sitting trot, the riders are asked to show a "shoulder-fore," which is a warm up for the shoulder-in. In the shoulder-fore, the horse remains in two-track movement, getting the suggestion of shoulder-in. "Just give him the idea of moving his body." As one of the horses slows down in evasion, Bill reminds the rider to go forward first before moving the horse's body against the outside rein. Bill uses the shoulder-fore as a limbering exercise for the horse and as a teaching aid for the rider. "Most times, people don't really understand how the three tracks work. But once they've begun to feel the sideways motion, it's easier to teach them."

The riders move up to the three-track movement of the shoulder-in. Again, Bill cautions them to remember forward motion. "Like anything else you do—jumping a fence or making a halt—always make sure the horse is in front of your legs."

Another change of direction comes at the posting trot. Bill asks them to show the different transitions within the trot from the ordinary trot to the working trot to the medium trot and, finally, the extended trot. One horse raises his head in resistance. "When you feel him go above the bit, that's his way of not accepting leg. When he goes above the bit, don't try to pull his head down. Instead, follow him up, keep the push until he starts to give a little bit. You can never get in trouble with a horse in front of your legs. You get in trouble when the horse is behind the rider."

With each increase in pace, Bill works with the students to teach them use of leg and to teach the horse acceptance of that pressure. "Don't give up asking him. Keep asking him until he starts to lengthen his trot. The more you ask him, the steadier your contact with the reins should be. Little spurts of speed will help teach him." Bill tells the riders to make sure the horses extend without being bent to one rein or the other.

A walk break is given, during which the riders cross their stirrups over the saddle. Bill explains to me that to win today in the equitation ring, rideability is the most important factor. The horses must only do what they are told, when they are told it. He reminds his students that they are forever schooling their horses to increase the horses' education and flexibility. He admits that as a professional he hasn't stopped watching what others do and says the depth of his teaching comes from his continuing interest in increasing his knowledge.

Starting up again, Bill asks the riders to show a haunches-in at the walk. He points out that this exercise is a great way for the rider to understand diagonal aids, which in turn locks in their understanding of how to always pick up the correct lead. Further, he says, the haunches-out is an exercise that teaches the counter canter. "Anytime you make haunches-in or a half pass, you want to make sure the horse is going more forwards than sideways. So when you go to position your horse, don't lock up on him [with your arms]. Make sure the horse can use his head and neck. Locking your arms can cause a horse to toss his head in resistance and cause him to move more and more into your leg." He reminds the riders to give a little when they feel the horse perform the exercise. Not a big release, but a softness through the arm that is a reward. "Move the horse's body against your inside rein . . . the braking rein is your outside rein, your bending rein is the inside rein. You should feel the haunches in advance of the shoulder."

Without irons, the riders move up to the sitting trot and show the haunches-in at the new gait. "Your elbows and arms should be like a door hinge. When he gives, you give," Bill reminds. The riders move naturally into the left lead canter. One rider is not as close to the saddle as Bill would like. He works with this rider in getting depth to her seat through a position correction and he tells her, "A sign of a good rider is a person who is connected to the horse, a person who is able to influence the horse through seat and leg."

He asks the riders to show the haunches-in at the canter on the circle. "You are making one circle one size with their front legs and one circle a smaller size with the hind legs." Bill has the riders go back out on the big circle before he asks them to make a smaller, tighter circle that will precede a change of direction. "Tighten the circle, almost so he is going into pirouette." The riders are now tracking right on the left lead. As each student performs the change of direction, Bill watches carefully to see that they don't lose their position and that the horse responds only to the rider's command. "Remember, the best rider is the rider who can influence the horse through seat and legs. If you can do that with great style, then you are the winner."

The students make another left-handed circle with a haunches-in to change direction. To see that his juniors understand diagonal aids, Bill asks each to show a flying change at a specific spot in front of him. Behind him they are to do a simple change to the counter lead before showing the flying change again. This exercise is to reinforce the use of opposite hand and leg to signal the appropriate lead. The students work on the exercise until the change signals are clear to the horse and performed promptly, from back to front. Bill is working too on reminding the horse that he must keep an evenness of stride through the changes and pay attention to the rider.

Bill tells me that his riders do more flat work than jumping work at home. He feels that the showing horses don't need the extra jumps. Additionally, he has found that prolonged flat work coupled with jumping is asking too much of the horse and rider's concentration. His horses are important to him. I heard a parent once remark that if given another life, she would like to come back as one of his show horses; they work, but are fussed over and cared for better than any of us humans.

Jumping

"Equitation is nothing more than good riding. Too much of our system promotes the cosmetic aspects. Too much stress is put on position. I favor the natural obstacles for schooling because they are an exposure that promotes growth in the rider's ability."

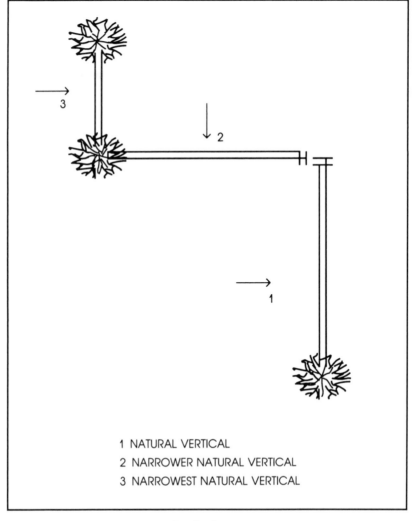

1 NATURAL VERTICAL
2 NARROWER NATURAL VERTICAL
3 NARROWEST NATURAL VERTICAL

Snake Jump

A small snake jump is the first exercise. The riders are to trot the first leg, canter the second and make the tight turn to the third, very narrow, leg. This exercise incorporates constant changes of direction, keeping the horses supple and ensuring the riders use both reins. It is more a study in balance and track than a study in pace. The short approach to the third, and most narrow, leg tricks the riders at first. "You don't need pace for this turn, you need your horse balanced and to the outside." The riders have to make sure the horses don't fall in on the turns; they have to keep to the track. Bill says they do more practice over the natural obstacles than they do ring work. It keeps the horses and riders fresher and teaches the riders independence.

The next exercise involves galloping to a hedge between two trees. The riders are to gallop away from us, over the hedge, execute a half-turn and return to it in the opposite direction. This is followed by a sweeping turn to the right and a gallop up the side of the bank to a small vertical off center at the top, to a canter down the drop side. If that goes well, and the riders are satisfied with the horses' responses at the top of the bank, they are to come back on the bank in the other (and harder) direction where the jump is closer to the edge. Bill warns his students, "I don't want to see the gallop pace let your eye get too long."

By forcing the riders to pick up the galloping pace, Bill is stretching their eye and their ability to see distances more quickly. He points out that the courses at most horse shows don't ask questions of the riders. It is not until the finals that the riders face the big questions. And without practice, it is too late for the rider to have the answer. He also favors the faster pace as it teaches the juniors not to worry so much about the perfect distance. "The horse shows make them very distance conscious, but once they get over the hump of pace, of the fear of making a mistake with their eye, it all gets easier for them. It makes them much more relaxed about their eye and the horses relax too." Bill watches rider position, noting that although he pretty much allows the riders to find their own balance up and down the slopes, he does want them to ride up the bank with a closed hip angle and down the hill with a more open angle.

The riders move on to a dry-ditch step jump up a fairly steep incline. From that jump they are to turn right and ride the open-ditch jump that is set in front of a two-rail vertical. I ask Bill how he tells riders to find a distance to a jump such as the second one. He tells me that

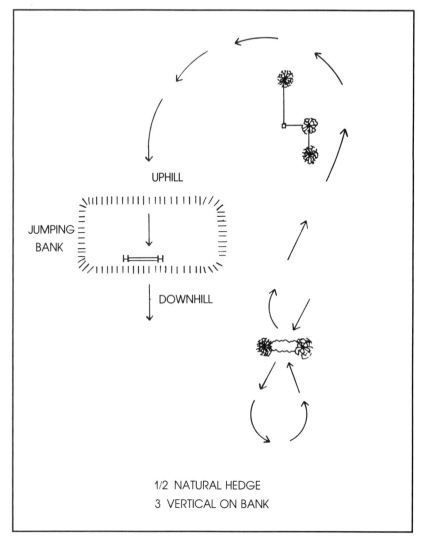

UPHILL

JUMPING
BANK

DOWNHILL

1/2 NATURAL HEDGE
3 VERTICAL ON BANK

First Course

most often he simply advises them to ride forward to a deep distance. If they need more information, he suggests they look at the lip of the ditch to determine the base of the jump.

"I'd say they do these natural jumps about forty percent of the time. Even if we have a ring course set, they'll warm up over these and then maybe walk to the sand ring and jump a course once or twice, and that's it. After all, how many times can a horse just jump around a ring without being bored?"

The riders show me an oxer liverpool jump. The permanent jump has the liverpool centered under the oxer so it sticks out just a couple of feet on both sides. They all jump this easily, moving on to the next challenge, which is the bank in the front-to-back (the long direction) approach. They have to jump up on one level, up to the next, and gallop down the sloping back side. Then they are to return with the sloping side first and the two tiers downward. The confidence that comes from mastery of the natural obstacles is becoming apparent in both the horses and the riders, who are having great fun.

A water jump is next. It has a rail over it to keep the horse's flight. The greenest horse is given a lead by a more experienced horse and both jump it the first time with no problem. Bill warns the rider on the green horse not to take the horse's willingness for granted as she returns on the jump. "The second time is always the worst—they actually know what they are jumping."

Lauren Hough returning on dry-ditch jump

Kym Ketcham

Lauren Hough jumping down the bank

Challenging the rider and the horse is a part of the value of natural obstacles. The grob is a place a rider must not jump ahead of the motion, and it is a place where the horse must learn to respond to command, even if the jump is spooky. There are no jumps set down in today's grob, just a water at the lowest point. One rider finds her horse uncertain about this obstacle. She gives the balky horse no option but to find his way through. Repetition creates further confidence for horse and rider.

Bill likes to end the natural work with a combination. He feels that it makes the horse "work his jump." Where the horses have been jumping "pretty stretched out," they need to remember collection. The combination in this case is a 25-foot in-and-out set at about 3′9″. Although the combination is made of oxers set around natural hedges, the similarity to a ring exercise is greater, and one rider reverts to her

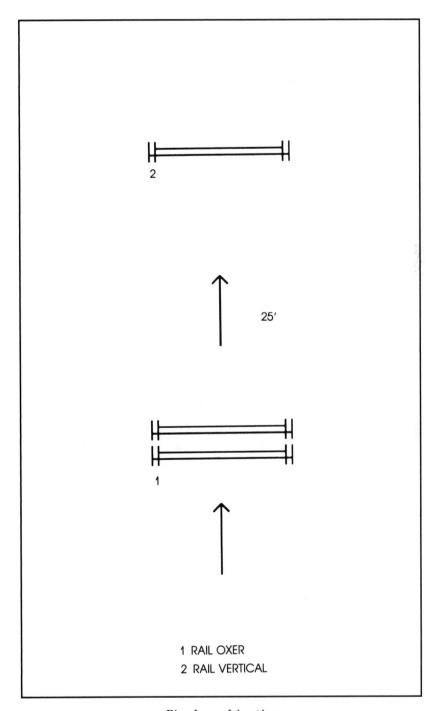

Final combination

show mentality of having to find the perfect distance. Pointing out her mistake, Bill tells me, "That's what too much ring work can do to them, it makes them timid. I find riding the natural jumps makes the riders braver, the horses braver. I think it makes the riders more independent. It makes their instinct for finding a good jump much better because it is so much more important out here."

Lauren Hough over the first element of the combination

Bill admits that all teachers try to protect riders from making mistakes even when they know mistakes are the best teacher. "We are all victims and all guilty of perpetuating a system that has homogenized our riders. There is too much repetition in today's show ring and few challenges. It causes us to turn out too many antiseptic riders. I tell my students that a good rider has the dedication and focus to move on past defeat to the next thing. A good rider gets the job done. The winning rider is the one who gets the job done with style. To prepare students for the big rings, you always have to be pushing and stretching them a little at a time."

❏ *Clinic and lesson information can be obtained by contacting Bill Cooney, North Street at Conyers Farm, Greenwich, CT 06381; 203-273-8003.*

FRAN and JOE DOTOLI

"It's either a discussion of pace or a discussion of direction."

Cannell

FRAN DOTOLI STUDIED RIDING UNDER ELAINE MOFFAT AND THE LEGENDARY GORDON WRIGHT. JOE DOTOLI RODE AS BOTH A JUNIOR AND AMATEUR BEFORE THEY OPENED YOUNG ENTRY IN 1969. TOGETHER THEY HAVE TURNED OUT SOME OF THE BEST RIDERS: PETER WYLDE, WENDY BAR-QUIN, JULIANNE TAYLOR, DAUGHTER ANN, ANDREA MOORE, AND MIA WOOD TO NAME A FEW. THESE RIDERS HAVE ACCOUNTED FOR MANY WINS IN THE EQUITATION CLASSES, INCLUDING THE FINALS. IN ADDITION, THEY HAVE TRAINED TOP HORSES, AMONG THEM BARYSHNIKOV, CATCH OF THE DAY, NATIVE SURF, PAY THE PIPER, LEGENDARY, AND DEVIL'S RIVER. BOTH FRAN AND JOE ARE AHSA JUDGES AND ARE OFTEN ON THE ROAD JUDGING SHOWS SUCH AS DEVON, THE HAMPTON CLASSIC, WEST PALM BEACH, THE ARIZONA CIRCUIT, AND THE GOLD CUP. FRAN IS A MEMBER OF THE AHSA ZONE 1 COMMITTEE AND THE AHSA EQUITATION COMMITTEE. JOE IS A CO-CHAIR OF THE NEW ENGLAND EQUITATION COMMITTEE. CURRENTLY FRAN & JOE MANAGE THE OX RIDGE HUNT CLUB FACILITY IN DARIEN, CONNECTICUT.

The Flat

"**I** like to think that my system is a building-block approach, that I teach in terms of exercises and mental pictures." Fran prefers teaching small lessons when working with the advanced students. This way she can customize a lesson to the student. "Some people are more visual, while others might better understand concepts in mathematical terms." Her point, that all of us process information differently, is one reason she prefers small lessons that enable her to address concepts in terms the riders will understand. "You have to be flexible" to find the best way to communicate to your students. Joe concurs, saying, "All riders won't fit one mold. One of the mistakes that people make is trying to bunch students up in one system. You can't treat them all the same. With ten riders of any age, you have ten different personalities. They all have their own style, both physically and emotionally. If you have a child or amateur who is really timid, the mounting of that rider is most important. That gives them time in the ring to breathe without having a disaster." Joe says the appropriate mounting of the riders is a huge part of a trainer's job.

Overall, Fran tries to simplify a problem or concept into two parts. "It's either a discussion of pace or a discussion of direction. Pace covers the gait and the speed at which you are going—collection or extension, for example. Direction would be going from point A to point B, the bend you might want, or the counter bend, for example." Like most of the top trainers, Fran explains they frequently get juniors in their last year of equitation showing, and all too often she discovers significant gaps in their basic training. "They will have been told to 'ride' their horse, which is far too vague an instruction for them to understand." She finds that the juniors get a lot of confidence from the ability to perform very exacting exercises correctly. "Once they get that confidence they can be led to exercises that give options and they have the faith in themselves to handle them."

Both Fran and Joe have teaching backgrounds, and that enables them to approach the sport from a different viewpoint. They try not to introduce new concepts to a student at a horse show and want their students to think of a show as a quiz, not a final exam.

Fran begins the flat work by having the students circle in front of her rather than around her. She likes keeping the riders in front of her so she has an unrestricted view of their work. Fran is one of many top trainers who dislikes ring work, preferring instead a big field for flat work. "I go back to Gordon Wright, who said if you have a field with a log in it, you have all you need."

The students have been asked to walk and trot, changing gaits every six or eight strides. "I watch them become more creative in getting their horses to become more accordion-like. At this level, I don't spoon-feed my riders, I like to see what they are doing with their horses. I give them a general exercise only and then watch and help them figure it out." The riders are encouraged to add changes of direction to the walk-trot work. During the exercise, Fran reminds them to hold their positions and suggests ways to make the transition smoother.

After a walk, they trot to the right, taking stock of their positions. "Let's have a little position check. Straight line from your ear to your shoulder to your hip to your heel." One of the horses is very fresh for this lesson and looking to invert and play. Fran shows me how the simplification of her system works with a problem. "If pace isn't working, try the directional solution. Try a little left bend and then slip him over to the other one." At the sitting trot, the fresh horse continues to be silly. Fran offers suggestions rather than orders. She wants the rider to figure out how to get the horse's attention and obedience. "Try right rein, left leg and see what you get. It's too much if he canters. Perhaps you want to try closing your left thigh on him more." All of the corrections are directional ones, since pace is not the problem.

After a rising trot across the diagonal, both students are asked to show a walk transition and then a canter. The fresh horse is much calmer in the new direction. They are asked for a trot transition, being careful not to let their bodies get ahead of the motion as they move forward in gait. They sit the trot, reversing direction again. As soon as the riders circle right, the fresh horse renews his resistance. "He's better to the left, correct? So, as I suggested before, you might try getting him in the left bend [the counter bend] and then slowly slide him over. He can do that."

Walk-canter-walk transitions are next, again working on the student's ability to rate her horse's speed and stride. Fran encourages her riders to vary their flat work so the horses don't get bored with the work. "I do feel the flat work is more important than the jumps; the junior horses have to be broke to death, but you don't want them to get sour." It is important to Fran that her students do not think of the horse as a disposable item. She wants them to be horsemen, knowing the animal and being fair with it. "Winning is about being consistent in competition. I want the kids to finish their junior years wishing they had another year, not relieved it's over."

Jumping

"It's human nature to practice what we do well, so I ask them to practice what they don't do well." This lesson is taped at a horse show with limited access to the jumps, since competition is going on around us. Nevertheless, Fran is able to set two jumps that give me a good idea about her pace and direction theory.

"There are really three paths to get from fence number one to fence number two. The inside turn, the middle road and the outside approach. We will go back and forth off different leads, planning ahead which path we will take and how pace will be affected by the path. With two fences set this way you can have any number of possibilities. It's track and how it reflects in pace and direction." For example, if the rider is asked to ride the inside, direct line, she will have to modify her steering and her pace to fit the required number of strides in.

Fran says that this type of exercise gives the riders confidence, as they are able to control pace and direction. From this she would have them think about finding a similar problem in a competitive situation. "Say this walks in a three and you need to get that in an equitation class, how would you address that problem? Or say it is the finals and you are meant to trot the second one. How would you address your pace and direction to that need? That is how it is a building block to the problems of the ring."

On this topic, Fran says she tries hard not to separate hunters from jumpers from equitation. "I feel they are sometimes too boxed. Nowdays too many people separate a horse into a category—he's a hunter or an equitation horse or a jumper. There are lots of similarities. But Fran says she notes that in years past, trainers would look at a horse

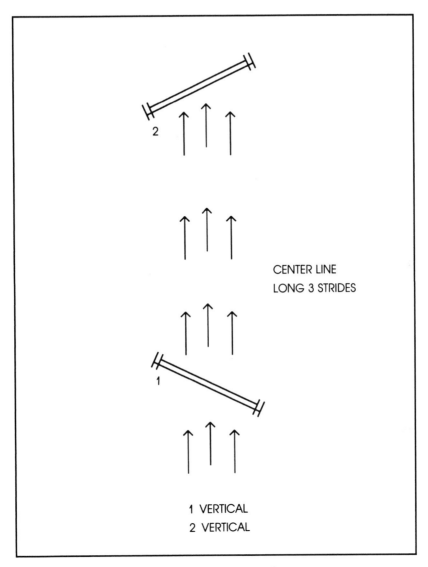

CENTER LINE

LONG 3 STRIDES

1 VERTICAL

2 VERTICAL

Optional Line Exercise

with a flat jump and say, "That's an equitation horse" because that type of jumper would allow a "starched child to sit up there and pose." She doesn't think that is true anymore. "If you took a look at the recent equitation finals and watched the horses competing in them, you would have seen some very good athletes, some good jumping-type animals." She feels judges are remiss if they don't penalize riders who consistently make their horses jump poorly, even if they get the right numbers down a line. She also believes riders should cross enter divisions as much as possible.

The students are asked to show us the middle-road track in three strides between the two jumps. Both riders misjudge and get four strides the first time. They need to correct through their pace. Once that is accomplished, they are asked to show four strides on the same track. Now they have to figure out how to downsize the pace to fit in four even strides. "Your direction is fine, but your pace is too much for this job."

After this they are asked to show the outside track in five strides. Once accomplished, they are asked to do the same exercise off the other lead. One rider is told to do five to teach her horse to collect, while the other is told to do four so her horse can learn to flow. "If you're getting there too early to the second jump and you already have him collected, what else can you do? Keep him to the right side. He's cutting in and jumping the left side of the second jump. So that's a problem with what? Direction, right?" Fran explains that the rider was trying to do the conservative number in the direct route, which wasn't going to work. She needed to change her direction—her route.

The riders demonstrate their ability to change from three to five strides, depending on their pace and direction. It is their job to figure out how much of their aids they need today to get the job done. The fresh horse gets three strides instead of four during one pass at it. "A good mistake would be to get five strides instead of three," Fran says, watching the horse drift left upon landing from the first jump. A good mistake. Too many juniors are afraid to make mistakes and yet there are good mistakes.

At home, the riders would perhaps do this exercise and then ride out of the jumping area to another field and back again to do the exercise a different way. "It's a point of discipline. It's an easy habit to make; to let the ring ride the horse rather than the rider riding the horse. "I like them to ride in and out of the defined area." Another exercise she uses at home comes from her background with Gordon Wright, who would put a bottle on a wide coop jump and have her jump it over and over until she could place the horse so that one leg was on each side of the bottle. "I don't use a soda bottle, but I might use a kerchief or something to teach them to place the horse." She feels that we can challenge the riders much sooner, so they are able "to know where they are on a line rather than relying on counting the numbers of steps."

Understanding competition is one of the biggest lessons a trainer has to teach. Fran and Joe start with a family meeting at the beginning of each show year where the goals are talked about as well as the sacrifices needed to reach those goals. "We try to keep an open dialogue." In order to excel you do have to practice and do well, but she says there are other obligations in life. Fran finds that students who have other interests gain the confidence that is needed in the ring. "You can experience adolescence and have a successful riding career. One shouldn't give up the school experience to show. It's work, but you can have it all. I think for riders to miss school, and miss the family life, puts a tremendous amount of stress on them. I think this is a great life for the kids as long as the whole family is involved."

Joe says that hard work and "connecting with the horse" are two paths to success. At Young Entry, under Dotoli's ownership, the students were expected to commit to their horses, spending time grazing them, bathing them, rubbing on them, playing with them. "It is important that they know their horses if they are to succeed. No matter who you are, if you want to win, it will take hard work. I mean every day, not just every two weeks." Joe elaborates, "Too many riders don't know how hard it is. It's not just riding around a ring. You have to know when you are working and know when you are pleasure riding and not confuse the two. Time with a horse will improve your performance." Joe further states that riding has many rewards that come from challenging your mental and physical abilities. And that "mental alertness" is a necessary ingredient to winning in the ring.

Judging

Both Fran and Joe are popular judges so we sat down and discussed some of the perceptions they have from the platform view.

"Every judge is looking for a good ride but some riders don't believe that," says Fran, shaking her head in wonderment. "I guess it's easier to place blame for ring nerves or low placings on someone besides yourself." Fran says she would like more exhibitors to view the judge as a friend, or an ally. As someone looking for the best you have to offer. Exhibitors should not ride into the ring as if the judge were the enemy. "I like to see a confident rider come into the ring, make a moment of eye contact with me and have the bearing that says, 'Look what I can do.' If the big trainers seem to get more of the blue ribbons, it's because their riders do better, not because of the trainer's name." As Fran points out, logically, big-name trainers got that way because of their successes, not their failures.

Joe says first he looks to see how the rider is affecting the horse, not whether the rider has a heel deeper than the ocean or a back straighter than an I-beam. "How they affect the horse is getting more and more paramount all the time to separate them [the winners from the losers]. He looks for a rider who "rides forward and straight. I don't like to see them picking their way around the jumps." By forward, Joe refers to having the horse in front of the rider's leg.

A word often used to describe a winner is "presence," that hard-to-detail quality that the top juniors have and are able to transmit to the judges. It is partly "grace under pressure," partly "confidence," partly "smoothness." It's a body language that says, "You want to watch me." More specifically, Joe says it is a solid softness rather than stiffness. "I would rather see a rider who is maybe not built in the classic form but who can melt into the jumps, who looks relaxed and can ride a horse forward, than a rider with long legs stiffly posed over the jumps."

In the hunter ring, the ultimate performance to Joe is one where "the rider can show the horse is balanced on his own. The rider should be able to balance the horse in the turns and then put a little bag in the reins to float down the line. There aren't too many riders who can do that. That's the ultimate. That's the perfect hunter ride." That ride is not what Joe wants to see in the equitation ring. Due to the nature of the distances in the equitation classes he looks for "the contact maintained, and that the horse is guided through each phase of the line."

Judging equitation and hunters is subjective, just as competitive ice skating or gymnastics are. There are deductions for small errors, larger deductions for larger errors, and few have ever received a perfect score. The best of our judges are professional horsemen and women who have stood on both sides of the ingate. They know the difficulties of both jobs. Joe admits that "certain characteristics of horses or riders will either drive you crazy or you'll love them. That's human nature."

It is much the same in all life, we pick our friends not because they are perfect, but because on some plane we are comfortable or enriched by them. So it is with judges. "George Dawson [a premier judge and trainer of horsemanship] once said to me that all judges judge according to the horses and riders that they've had." Joe agrees, pointing out this makes for many different opinions in judging. "That's why one horse can be champion one week and maybe not win the tri-color the next week. It doesn't affect the important basic things like rails down, bad form, lost leads and such, but when you need a tiebreaker, it is your personal experience that tips the scale one way or the other." Joe feels this is good for the industry.

Both Fran and Joe agree the opening circle is vital. It is the first impression you make on the judge. Keeping a judge waiting or rushing through the introduction are extremes that are not show worthy; the opening circle should be "tidy, neat and businesslike." Fran says she sees too many exhibitors who look like they'd rather be someplace else, and Joe agrees, saying the rider who gets his attention is the one who rides in, saying through body language "Look at me, I'm something special." When the Dotolis are judging, they like to see a brief eye contact from the rider, saying it gets their attention even at the end of a long, tiring, day.

During the course itself, both Fran and Joe agree that they are looking for a soft, strong trip. "Like a ballerina: they are very strong, muscled dancers, yet their dancing looks very soft and fluid. That's what a good rider should be able to do." Also during the course, they both watch to see how mistakes are handled. "There will always be something" that doesn't go perfectly. And, they admit, it helps to be mounted on a nice horse. The overall picture is one of a partnership and the two parts should fit.

The judging doesn't end with the last jump. It ends when you leave the ring. That means attention to the closing circle and presentation too.

When it comes to testing equitation riders, both have their favorite tests. They choose tests that highlight pace problems, such as showing a halt within a line, and they like to use directional problems, such as jumping the out of an in-and-out. Fran likes to bring the riders to be tested into the center of the ring so they have to think on their own.

And when it's over? "We don't measure success in ribbons," Joe

Ellen Raidt-Lordi

Ann Dotoli demonstrating ring presence

says. "Horse showing is about horses, not ribbons." Instead, as trainers, they look to see if the rider has attained his/her goal in relationship to getting what is needed from the horse. Fran believes "the ring is a reflection of the lessons rather than a ribbon."

❑ *Clinic information can be obtained by contacting Ox Ridge Hunt Club, P.O. Box 1067, 512 Middlesex Road, Darien, CT 06820; 203-655-2559.*

KAREN HEALEY

"There is no 'bad' distance."

Tish Quirk

KAREN HEALEY WORKED FOR GEORGE MORRIS FOR FOUR AND A HALF YEARS BEFORE TAKING OVER THE HEAD TRAINER RESPONSIBILITIES AT TEWKSBURY FARM, WHERE SHE STARTED RUTH ANN BOWERS, KIM BENZEL, FREDDY AND DAISY WELLS AND OTHER GREAT JUNIORS. IN 1981 SHE MOVED TO CALIFORNIA AND HAS BEEN PRODUCING WINNERS EVER SINCE. RIDER LAUREN KAY WON THE 1990 ALFRED B. MACLAY FINALS (AFTER PLACING SEC- OND THE YEAR BEFORE), WON THE USET FINALS AND PLACED IN THE AHSA MEDAL. RIDER MEREDITH MICHAELS CAME EAST FOUR CON- SECUTIVE YEARS AND PLACED IN THE MEDAL AND MACLAY EVERY TIME. CARLEE MCKAY WAS THE RESERVE CHAMPION IN THE 1991 MACLAY FINALS, PLACED FOURTH IN THE MEDAL, WON THE ASPCA WEST COAST REGIONALS AND THE AHSA ZONE 10 HUNT SEAT MEDAL FINALS. BLAKE SCHLEI, AMY WYMER AND LISA OSIER ALSO HAVE CONSISTENTLY WON THE BIG CLASSES. AND KAREN HAS TRAINED SOME OF THE TOP HUNTERS IN THE COUNTRY. THE 1988 AHSA RESERVE HORSE OF THE YEAR WENT TO HER FIRST-YEAR GREEN ENTRY, TRUMP CARD. THE 1990 AHSA HORSE OF THE YEAR WAS AWARDED TO MAGIC WORD, WHO WAS ALSO THE GRAND HUNTER CHAMPION (JUNIOR HUNTER) OF THE NATIONAL HORSE SHOW IN 1991. KAREN WAS VOTED CALIFORNIA PROFESSIONAL HORSEMAN'S ASSOCIATION HORSEWOMAN OF THE YEAR IN 1991 AND CURRENTLY SERVES AS THE CHAIR OF THE PACIFIC COAST EQUITATION COMMITTEE. SHE IS A MEMBER OF THE PACIFIC COAST HORSE SHOWS ASSOCIATION (PCHSA) BOARD OF DIRECTORS IN ADDITION TO HER DUTIES AS A COMMITTEE MEMBER OF THE AHSA IN THE JUNIOR HUNTER, HUNTER AND EQUITATION DISCIPLINES.

The Flat

"**L**earning to ride is easy. If you follow the steps, success soon follows." Karen believes everyone can learn to ride, and her lessons are geared to riders at all levels. Her only concession to differing abilities are the heights of the jumps and the level of mastery she expects. Her system is "firmly rooted in flat work and basic dressage." As she will tell you, "By controlling the horse's speed, his balance and the track, the rider can and must learn to make any distance work." She explains to me that there is no "bad" distance. There might be a poorly rated or a poorly balanced horse off the track, but that doesn't have to be. Control those variables and you have success. And she doesn't believe in allowing the rider to depend on lots of fancy equipment to get the job done. "I see far too much of the artificial hardware out there: gogues, chambons, gimmicky bits." That, she believes, is a search for the quick fix. Not a search for learning how to ride. She is interested in making riders, not in dispensing Band-Aid solutions.

Her riders are mounted on big thoroughbreds, which she prefers for the show ring. "They can usually be trained more easily without the gimmicks—especially by young girls." Each horse is bitted in a snaffle bit, and no martingale is used.

The lesson this day begins with walk work. Karen explains the objective of the lesson is "controlling and riding a specific track to a distance." She reminds the riders the lesson will require the use of both hands and both legs. In a clinic situation, Karen will often begin by working walk-halt transitions because it is her experience that most riders let their horses run through their hands. She says "that causes most of the bad jumps on course. I often spend time walking and halting to assess the horse's reaction. The horse's response should be immediate, and the rider should give as soon as the horse does. It's very much a punishment/reward system."

As our four riders walk, Karen reminds them to "Feel the horse walking from your leg to your hand. Not hurried, not rushed. When you close your leg they shouldn't walk through your hand, they should move up to your hand." She is also reminding the riders to be accurate and precise about the bend and track they seek. Just as Karen doesn't let her riders off the hook, so the riders should not let their horses off the hook. At the walk, the riders are asked to bring the horses to a haunches-in position. "Ride all four corners of the horse. You can't control direction without controlling the haunch. Think of it as pushing a wheelbarrow along a set of tracks. You are pushing, not pulling." The riders then demonstrate a haunches-out and repeat the two positions to gain flexibility of their horses.

A posting trot is picked up next, with the same warning to make sure the horse is moved from leg to hand. The students are reminded to keep the trot a two-track movement and not allow the hind end to find a third track. "Create a chute to control the track. Using both hands and both legs, keep him within the chute. As you put him around your inside leg, your outside hand balances. Keep your hands about five inches apart. If you lock your hands together, the chute gets too narrow and you can't control the shoulders. If your hands are too far apart, you give the horse license to wander."

The riders change direction through a half turn and ride a forward trot "without hurrying." Each rider is asked to show an individual circle where they "control the haunch with leg and control the shoulder with hand." A broken line at the sitting trot follows, which is a place for the rider to feel how she influences the haunch with the alternating bends. Karen asks them to continue the exercise showing her more pace. "You have to be able to control the track at speed too," she informs them.

Karen likes to use the analogy of driving as it pertains to riding. She is fond of having her riders think of steering the horse with as little effort as they steer their cars. "When you drive a car you don't stare down at the hood. Your eye works ahead and you automatically turn the steering wheel where you need to go. The use of eye triggers an automatic response from your body."

The riders are asked to rise to the trot and show an extension of stride across the diagonal of the ring. It is important that variations of pace be practiced so the rider is adept at holding track at all speeds. After performing three extensions, they are instructed to collect their horses and perform the haunches-in. "Don't hold your horse up with your hand. Feel his hind end come underneath you." They go to working on a circle with the haunches in, "putting him around your inside leg." The riders alternate extension exercises with collection work, all the time building their feel of placing their horses at the different speeds. After another half turn, they show us a half pass back to the track as Karen advises them to "Keep the left bend until you get to the track, then change to the new inside bend."

All the flat work is directly connected to the lesson of the day. In order for the rider to be able to control the track of the horse, she has to know how to control it, when to control it and how to maintain control at various stages in the upcoming courses. The most important thing a rider can do, according to Karen, is to be able to ride the track with both hands and both legs.

The horses are given a walk break before being asked to perform a turn on the hindquarters at that gait. Following that, they are asked to canter off into individual circles. Karen cautions the riders to sit still during the canter by staying relaxed. They repeat this exercise in obedience before showing a broken line at the canter with a simple change of lead at each change of bend. "Keep him around your inside leg, blocking him with your outside leg so his haunch stays directly behind the front end." These horses melt back to the walk in an instant, performing the simple change perfectly. "Now show me the broken line on the left lead . . . keeping the left lead all the time." This is a wonderful test of the horse's obedience to commands. Once each horse has performed it satisfactorily, the riders are asked to make a half-turn, which takes them to the left lead on the left circle. The riders are encouraged to lengthen the stride on the left lead before asking for collection and the haunches-in at the canter. "Now make a circle with the haunches in, a volte. Feel that he's short, he's light and he's balanced." After another chance to canter on the long side, the riders make a half-turn, changing direction without changing lead. At the counter canter, Karen asks them for a haunches-out. A flying change on the straightaway restores the horses to the correct lead, and they are allowed once again to extend. "When you lengthen, make sure the balance stays the same. Don't let him get heavier in the neck." The exercise is repeated in the opposite direction.

"Halt. Then show me a counter canter on the right circle. Hold his haunch . . . get him around your left leg." It is obvious that these riders are familiar and comfortable with this hard flat workout. Both the students and the horses are making this look very easy. "A broken line with flying changes now, and don't let them speed up or lengthen when you ask for the change. Make sure they don't start cutting in. Don't let them, shift the shoulder. When you have the lead, put them around your inside leg rather than letting them increase the pace."

Jumping

The first exercise is a circle of jumps set at a low height. The riders are to ride the track that will get them five even strides between all of the jumps. They are working simultaneously in a line. The idea of this exercise is to get the riders using both reins, both legs and their eyes to maintain track. In addition, the horses get supple by turning around the inside leg and rein. The exercise will not work if a rider stops her horse in the air. "I want her to shape her horse in the air." It is Karen's observation that the young riders of today either ride with the automatic (crest) release or no release at all. This turning exercise is meant to address that problem by teaching the rider to "jump out of hand" by following the motion of the horse and influencing it, while never, never stopping the forward movement.

She asks the riders to make sure they keep a separation between their hands and to address the problems of their individual horses. "If your horse falls in, use more outside rein and leg. If he is moving out off the track, bring him in. It is not the speed that is the issue here, it is the track. Make them stay to the exact track."

Once the riders maintain track and pace in one direction, they must do again in the opposite. Again, Karen makes use of the driving metaphor. "If you are riding the brake, you have to floor the gas pedal. Ease off the brake, relax the hand and you can ease off the gas." She tells me she likes this exercise because it teaches riders to use both hands and both legs, or else they can't have a comfortable jump. "Once they understand about track, I add pace, such as galloping on a bend. But that is difficult. First they have to get focused on putting the horse where they want it."

The second jumping exercise consists of a figure eight over two oxers, one of them a liverpool. The jumps are set close to the fence line so the riders are forced to ride the turns just before the jumps. The students work this two at a time, so they also have to monitor pace and watch out for the other rider crossing the line to the jump. She admonishes the students to keep the turns tight. "Get him around your

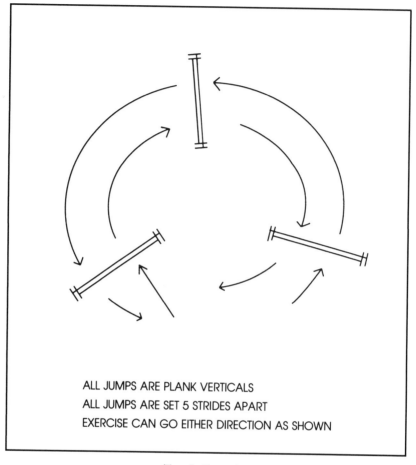

ALL JUMPS ARE PLANK VERTICALS
ALL JUMPS ARE SET 5 STRIDES APART
EXERCISE CAN GO EITHER DIRECTION AS SHOWN

Track Exercise

right leg. Don't let him off the track, get his hind end under you." Karen likes this exercise because it teaches the riders how to hold the horse out on a turn and how to use diagonal aids to perform it correctly. "Outside rein and inside leg will get him out on the turn, then outside leg and inside hand will bring him in to a specific place on the jump." It is another step in teaching the use of two hands and two legs. The short turn is the place she is most likely to see the rider mistake of jumping ahead. "Keep your weight as you see the distance. Don't go to the distance with your body."

On another day she might ask the riders to gallop on the long approach to a jump and then to show the single jump at various speeds,

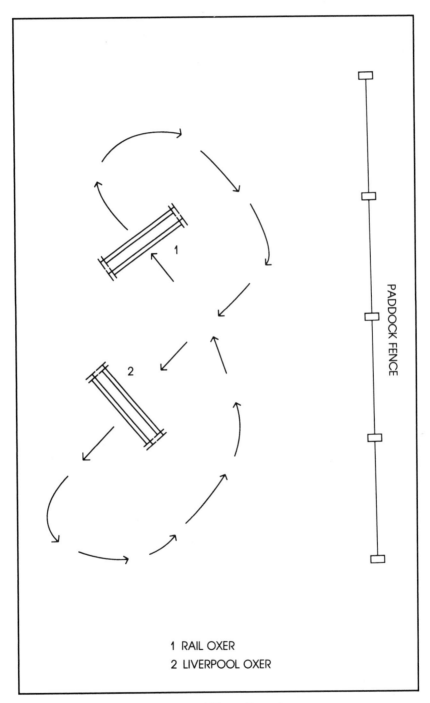

1 RAIL OXER
2 LIVERPOOL OXER

PADDOCK FENCE

Jump and Turn Exercise

but today she is demonstrating how to adhere to the track that presents the distance.

The third exercise involves the ability to turn to a "blind" jump, ride a bending six strides to a vertical, find the track over the vertical that will take the direct route to the liverpool in a direct six strides.

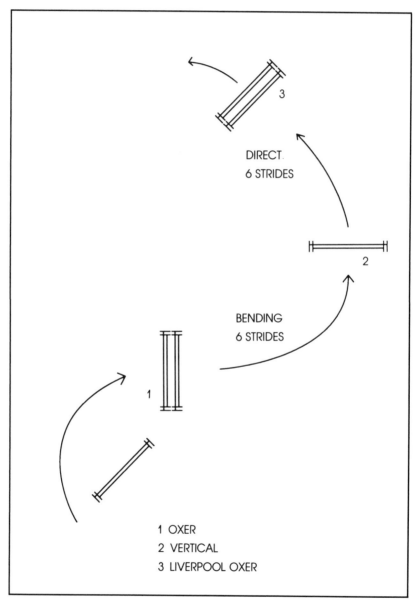

Bending to direct line exercise

"You'll have to get them off your left leg to your right hand. Your right hand will then create the track to the direct five." Despite her warnings about the first fence, one rider has trouble getting to it. "Control the shoulder but remember to give a little off the short turn." Karen favors setting oxers off short turns to teach riders to be comfortable with the closer distance. Often she will ask riders to counter canter low, wide oxers to help reinforce the same principle.

The fourth exercise builds on the previous three. The riders are faced with an skinny oxer to a bending line in an easy five to a full-size oxer. From this second oxer they must find the track that takes them in a direct five to a third jump that is a brush box with no standards. Because the first fence is narrow, it is not an easy jump to angle. It is important that the riders get the horse to the left side of fence 2 if they are to make the direct line to the last effort. They will have to be accurate since this jump has no wings to pull the horse toward the center. "It has nothing to do with speed," Karen advises, "but everything to do with track." One rider has difficulty keeping the track over the middle jump; her horse wants to drift left, and it causes a refusal at the last jump. "Draw a straight line with both hands, both legs and both eyes. Control the direction."

Once this is accomplished the exercise is altered to add pace as a factor. The riders are to ride the five strides in the first part and then move up for four strides in the second part. It is even more vital they keep to the track to accomplish the subtraction of a stride off a quiet first distance.

Finally, the riders have to show the same first line with a difference. They must be able to direct their horses to the right side of the second jump so they have room to make a bending line left to a blind jump. Now they have to angle the first jump some, in order to get to the right side of the oxer. The horse who likes to drift left finds this challenging. He has a wandering line between 2 and 3 and is surprised when he sees fence 3 in front of him. "He can't bend without your leg. You can't control his hindquarters without leg on him. You've got to follow a track that will get him to land to the right after the oxer. Your right hand becomes the balancing rein. You have to get him on the right rein around your left leg." As the rider works this out, Karen says this exercise is excellent for riders who tend to be worried about finding a tough first fence. "They get so worried about finding the first jump that they forget to find a track between the others. This teaches them

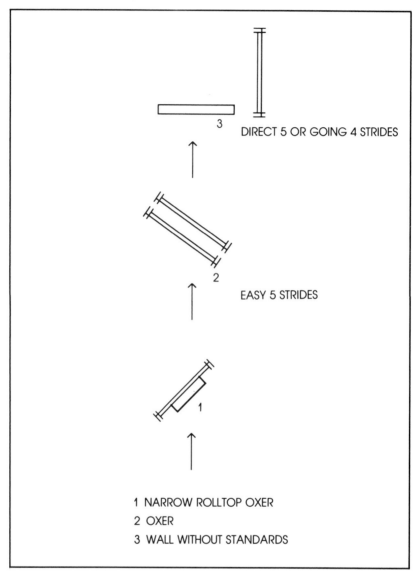

3 DIRECT 5 OR GOING 4 STRIDES

2 EASY 5 STRIDES

1 NARROW ROLLTOP OXER
2 OXER
3 WALL WITHOUT STANDARDS

Creating track in the air

to be aware of the relationships in a group of fences rather than focusing on just one tough one."

Karen always has her riders practice over very difficult patterns and exercises. She sees every course as a series of gymnastics, or exercises, and it's her goal to make sure her riders have seen everything possible at home and practiced it all until it flows.

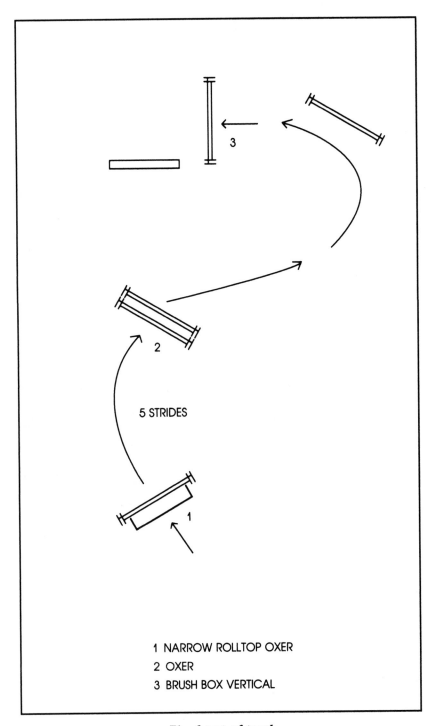

Final test of track

She tells me the hardest part of teaching students of top caliber is not the riding part. The most difficult thing is to teach the winners how to handle the pressures that accompany victory. "The riders must want success so badly they can taste it, but still they have to be able to channel that energy in a positive direction. They must learn from their mistakes but never accept them. They should never worry about beating other riders, only about beating themselves. They should know that each time they ride, whether in a show ring or a lesson, they should be better than they were the time before."

Lauren Kay, 1990 ASPCA Maclay winner, on Gulliver

Karen and I talked about the state of equitation today. She is encouraged that there are so many opportunities for the junior rider from the equitation finals to the Prix de State and Young Rider's competitions. It is a small world now, and even European experience is not outside the realm of some juniors. But Karen states, "I see too many people who don't learn to ride, they only learn to show." That is a problem

Tish Quirk

Carlee McKay, 1991 ASPCA Maclay reserve aboard Gulliver

we need to be aware of with the growing trend toward low-height jumper classes. "Children's jumpers has nothing to do with learning how to ride. I've seen many riders skip the equitation and go right into these three-foot jumper classes. They don't make it in the long run." Karen feels that equitation classes are the foundation on which great riders build. "They have to know the flat work, the basic figures."

What about the rider who has the talent but not the funds to train with a top trainer? "Nobody gave it to me. If you really want it, you will work to get it. You can be a working student, remembering that means hard work at less-than-glamorous jobs, and you can go to clinics. You should sit in the schooling areas at horse shows and listen to the best teachers. Really listen. There are many ways to work your way to the top."

❏ *Clinic information can be obtained by contacting Karen Healey Stables, P.O. Box 6872, Thousand Oaks, CA 91359; 805-523-8235.*

MIKE HENAGHAN

*"There are no mistakes—
there is just learning."*

Cannell

MIKE IS CURRENTLY THE TRAINER AT NEW-
STEAD FARM IN UPPERVILLE, VIRGINIA,
WHERE HE TRAINS THE FIRESTONE FAMILY
WHILE PRODUCING FINE HORSES. HIS
PATHS THROUGH THE EQUESTRIAN
WORLD HAVE BEEN MANY AND HAVE
TAKEN HIM FROM HIS EARLY HOME IN
CONNECTICUT TO THE MIDWEST, THE
SOUTHEAST, BACK TO THE NORTHEAST
AND OUT AGAIN. HE LEARNED FROM EU-
ROPEAN TRAINERS AND FROM GORDON
WRIGHT. HE HAS PASSED ON HIS CONSIDERABLE KNOWLEDGE TO RIDERS SUCH AS BEEZIE PATTON,
GREG BEST, NORMAN DELLO JOIO, JANE WOMBLE, EMIL SPADONE, ALAN BAZAAR, RAY TEXEL,
CHERYL WILSON AND DARREN GRAZIANO. MIKE'S STUDENTS ALSO GET THE BENEFIT OF THE WORK-
ING RELATIONSHIP HE HAS WITH HENRI AND KATIE PRUDENT, A RELATIONSHIP THAT ENABLES MIKE
TO EXPAND HIS TEACHING PROGRAM INTO THE JUMPER RANKS. IT IS PLANNED THAT SOME OF
MIKE'S STUDENTS WILL BE ABLE TO SPEND SUMMERS AT THE PRUDENT FARM OUTSIDE PARIS,
FRANCE.

The Flat

"**I** have a nonstructured approach to equitation," Mike tells me. "I find
safe, simple environments to correct faults rather than just repeating
the correction over and over. I think you get a much more versatile
rider. It's amazing to watch the students when they figure it out on

their own. A light bulb goes off." The enthusiasm Mike brings to his lessons is contagious, and he looks for students who exhibit excitement for learning. He stresses that his exercises do the teaching. But I found his communication skills to be expert.

In the lessons I was able to watch, Mike started all the riders off on a self-directed warmup. During this time he didn't want to see more than a stretching of muscles and an appraisal of the horse's attitude for the day. Mike sees riding as a partnership between horse and rider, and as you will see, he encourages the horse to do his share of the thinking.

"We'll spend a few minutes talking about what we want to accomplish on the flat, but I don't feel riders can take hours and hours of concentrated work, so they won't be having a flat lesson in the traditional sense. If a rider has a major problem on the flat, I think it should be addressed in a separate lesson." Mike urges the riders to test their mount's level of cooperation at this moment. "Is he willing? Is he dull? Is he sulky? How much leg will it take to get him to move forward today? How much hand will it take to get a response? These are the types of questions he asks his riders to consider as they warm up. Naturally, as he asks them for input, he is making his own judgments about the horse's mood and abilities.

Extending the evaluation, the riders are asked to begin demanding more from the horses. "Bring him to your aids, maintaining a rhythm like a metronome: bup,bup/bup,bup/bup,bup." He reminds the riders of basics as they get into the minds of their horses. "If you want to be soft, be soft from the arm, not from the open hand. From your shoulder, through your elbow, through your wrist," or "More weight in your heel." Reminding rather than carping.

Constantly asking questions of his students helps Mike know what their frame of reference is at any given time. This way he can guide their thinking toward the appropriate issues at hand. "What kind of trot do you have? What's going on underneath you?" His questions are tools for directing the rider's attention toward the horse.

When asking one of the riders to show him collection, the rider, afraid of making a mistake, errs on the side of caution. Because she is weak with her commands, she isn't able to get the job done. Mistakes are not the enemy to Mike. "Don't be afraid of making a mistake. If he breaks into a trot, you'll find out what it takes to collect him without losing him." Another rider is working on her dull horse, waking him up to her leg. Mike counsels her to use her cluck and her stick if necessary to make her point clear to the horse, at the same time urging the rider to keep up to pace.

Mike asks the riders to show lengthening and collecting work, changing the stride fairly frequently. "Pace is something we don't practice enough. We should practice about fifty percent on galloping work and about fifty percent on collected work. Too often the percentages are more like ninety percent collected and ten percent galloping. Then we wonder why horses get so excited when we finally let them gallop! We need to practice both more evenly, on the flat and over the jumps."

He encourages the riders to keep the rhythm as they ask for more from their horses. "Bup,bup/bup,bup/bup,bup, that metronome has always got to be in the back of your head. Shape the turns with the metronome working." Mike wants the riders to visualize their horses as seesaws. Depending on the individual horse and the job at hand, the horse can be ridden with the front end level, or slightly raised or even tipped down. To influence the front end, the students must influence the back end of the horse.

One rider is on a horse who tends to get low in front (on his forehand) when he lengthens stride. Mike works with this rider on raising one end of the seesaw. He suggests that she might want to work her horse on hills to help the horse find better balance. "Cantering down a hill forces the horse to slip his hind end underneath him. Lots of times when horses don't open and close without getting heavy, it's because they don't understand what we are asking: usually because the aids are conflicting. So what would benefit you, would be to create a natural environment for yourself where the horse does more of the work. It doesn't have to be a steep grade, but there is a lot you can do on a hill to teach balance and self carriage. Working on the hill, maybe do a circle in the middle of the downgrade or ask for a leg yield up the hill. Ask for a shoulder-in or a shoulder-out up and down hill. A hill accentuates the exercise, making the horse very conscious of his balance." Mike feels young riders today are disadvantaged by the decline of true hunt courses and the use of rolling fields as rings. For various reasons they ride most often on flat, safe surfaces. He feels that has contributed to a decline in riding skills. "When you work all the time on flat, prepared surfaces, the rider has to do ninety percent of the work during a lesson. When you work on hills, the horse does ninety percent of the work. As soon as a horse starts to fall on his front end, point him down a hill . . . he'll find his hind end very quickly. If you get a horse that is not pushing, point him up a hill. He'll have to push."

All of Mike's work is presented in terms of building toward a goal, not replacing one skill with another. During the flat work, he is teaching a student how to identify balance problems she may not be considering, while asking her to maintain the rhythm. "What is your horse doing? What about his lateral balance? Your first response should be with your inside leg, keeping the rhythm as you ask him for give from your leg." He has the rider demand simple flexion from the horse by taking the inside rein, reminding her that the rider always rides with two legs and two reins. "One leg or hand doesn't replace the other . . . it dominates the other." To prove this to the rider through an exercise, he asks her to pick two places on the circle where she will ask her horse to slow down, stepping his inside hind leg toward the outside rein. "First, two reins and two legs, straightness and rhythm. Then sit and ask him to shorten his stride and move his haunches toward the outside with the dominant inside leg." As they work, it becomes clear that on this day the horse is quite responsive to the rider's right leg and a little dull to the left. Mike explains what this will mean when it comes time to jump: "You know he's going to lay all over your left leg today."

The rider remarks that usually her horse is resentful to the right leg, and Mike notes that horses have a way of changing on us and warmup should be an evaluation of what you have that day, not what you had two weeks ago. He also says it is common for horses who have been corrected a great deal on one side to go to a stiffness on the other. That, he says, is why it is important to work both sides evenly.

Mike has two of his riders do the canter work from a half-seat. He asks for trot/canter/trot/canter transitions in the two-point position. He wants them to be able to control their horses in the position they'll use in the hunter ring. "Your aids should be just as proficient in the two-point. When you jump around a hunter course you have to stay pretty much where you are. The horse has to go forward without you having to sit down, and he's got to come back without you pulling for all you're worth." Obviously, the exercise also reinforces depth in heel and promotes a long leg contact.

He tells the riders to use their voices as an aid to help with the downward transition from canter to trot. Mike believes that horses should be responsive to hand aids, leg aids and voice aids. Adding collection and extension to the canter work, the rider is to remain in the two-point position. "Collect without sitting . . . then give again to lengthen. You are establishing with your horse the signals you will give and establishing your response to his behavior. This way you both know what to expect."

As they continue their work on collection and extension, Mike sees the riders aren't really getting collection; they are slowing their horses down. They are relying on pulling back with their hands without using leg. The reliance on the reins stops the horses' engines. "Show me a short horse at the canter. Show me short in his body. I want his stride to get shorter, but I also want to see his body get shorter. Don't be afraid of a trot, be tougher, tougher." Again, the riders are reminded to keep the metronome going in the back of their heads. "We have longer and shorter but we never have faster and slower. The rhythm stays the same while the stride changes. The rhythm is always there. This is a simple exercise to make you aware of the four corners of your horse and to remind you that no matter how you manipulate the horse laterally or longitudinally, you always have the sense of the horse carrying you."

The schooling area at a horse show is not the place to introduce complicated flat work. Mike believes new material is better learned in lessons and training sessions at home or on nonshowing days. The message he wants these riders to understand is that the schooling area is a place to assess and remind rather than teach. It is the place the rider can make judgments about the strengths and weaknesses of the day. It is a place to remind the horse of the signals that will be used in the ring and a place to make those signals very clear.

Jumping

The first exercise Mike demonstrates for me is one that he feels strongly about. Trust. Mike, more than many other trainers, believes the horse has an equal role to play in the partnership. Much of his teaching involves allowing and demanding the horse do his half of the work.

In order for the team to succeed, it is necessary that the team members trust each other.

He has set two very small plank jumps alongside a paddock fence in a small gully. "I want to see you jump the two planks with a very loose rein in a two-point position." The two students in this exercise find it very difficult. "I want you to do whatever strides the horse wants, I want you steering but not pushing . . . discipline yourself. You are allowing your horse to jump. We don't care if we chip . . . we are not working on distance." Both riders want to "help" their horses find the right strides. "It's very important for riders to learn confidence in their horses' abilities and in their horses' desire to do the job." The riders are struggling with self-control, trying to prevent the horses from rushing down the line to get there in a short stride. "If he gets four and a half strides and chips because he hasn't kept his stride even, let him! If he gets in dead wrong and has to reach for the second jump, let him! You are trying to make the horse concentrate on his job so he learns to do his fifty percent. If you want an attentive horse, you have to allow the occasional mistake." It is an exercise that teaches trust but also teaches the rider, out of necessity, to find the center of the horse and wait patiently.

The same conversation comes up in another lesson. In this case, the rider overrides a line getting her horse close to the second jump. When asked why she pushed her horse to the tight spot, she responds that she felt her horse was lagging behind her. "You are schooling. Let the jumps teach your horse something. If he doesn't listen to you in the line, he'll catch a rub at the oxer. Let him! He won't want to do it twice. Let him think a little bit. If you help him every time, he'll learn to depend on you and on the day you don't do everything right, you'll have a big problem as he says, 'Where were you? You've always been there before.' Don't overprotect your horse." Mike knows that horses don't need riders in order to jump. And he says, they don't need riders to tell them when to leave the ground. "A horse has an eye too; it's not just the rider. Horses see distances and they can judge height. We have to learn to trust that." With that trust comes better performance. "When a horse knows a particular rider won't suddenly change the rules in front of the jump, he'll really take over and start to help you all the time." Training is nothing if it isn't about teaching horses to respond to our signals, and Mike says a good, experienced horse knows

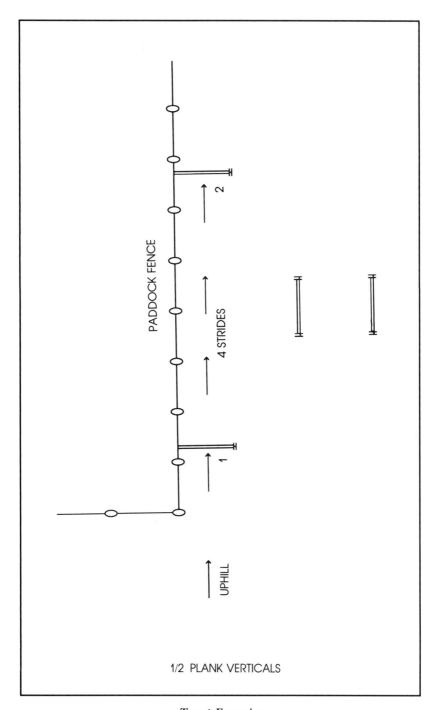

Trust Exercise

his job. "When you get on a good horse and pick up a gallop, he'll know he is looking for the big distance. Conversely, if he's collected and short, he knows he's going to canter the ground line."

The next exercise I witness is one to teach heels down and adherence to track. Using the plank jumps along a paddock rail in addition to a one-stride in-and-out set on a short but significant slope, the riders are given a small course that incorporates terrain with steering. The riders are to jump the plank jump, turn right going up the hill, catch the in-and-out, make a small left turn back to the plank line. They are told to get three strides between fences 1 and 2. Uphill proves easy. The test comes when the course is reversed and the in-and-out is ridden downhill to the short three strides. The exercise proves its mettle. The first rider doesn't get her weight in her heel, which forces her to land on the horse's neck. Since her horse drifts left and she is powerless in her current predicament, the horse gets two strides after the in-and-out, instead of three. The exercise has told her that she must land in her heel so she can balance herself, leaving her free to steer to the required track for the three strides. The next rider carries too little pace to the in-and-out, which makes the distance invisible to her. She gets left in the air. The exercise has shown her that distances come from pace while reinforcing a deep heel. This is an example of using an exercise and terrain to teach discipline. Mike did not have to stand in the ring calling out "Heels down," and the students learned quickly it was in their best interest to find their bases.

Another example of getting an exercise to solve a problem is demonstrated for me. This one is designed to help a novice rider know where she is on a line. The student claims her brain disconnects from her body as she rides down a line, and by the time she gets to the second fence, she has no idea where she is. Since she has already worked hard on the flat, learning to be aware of her horse's stride, she has a leg up on the exercise. She is first told to trot a small vertical into a line, canter seven strides out over the oxer at the end of the line and then halt. Mike picks her brain, asking her to identify the number of strides she got and the attitude of her horse towards the jumps. Was he aggressive? Passive? Weak? Did he pull? He reminds her, "There is no right or wrong here, I just want to see what you are aware of."

The rider accomplishes the exercise but feels flustered. "I can't count up to seven!" The cure comes with Mike asking her to break up the strides into two groups of her choice. They move to a line that

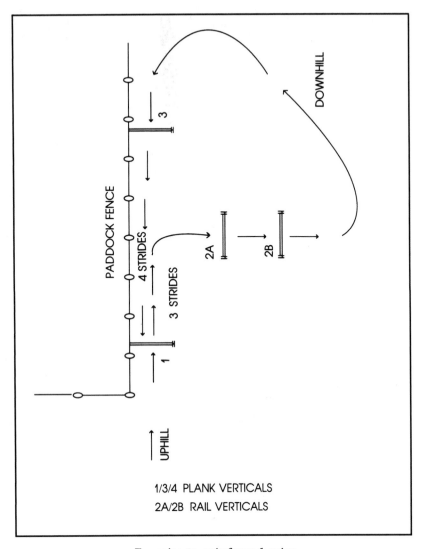

PADDOCK FENCE

DOWNHILL

4 STRIDES

3 STRIDES

UPHILL

1/3/4 PLANK VERTICALS
2A/2B RAIL VERTICALS

Exercise to reinforce basics

when trotted into will yield eight strides. This gives the rider a chance to break up her strides evenly into four and four. "Effect no change in the first four strides, then in the second four strides just see where you are."

Mike explains to me that he favors this solution to help riders find their way on a line. He tells me it gives the horse a chance to jump the first fence without interference from the rider and gives the rider a chance to relax for four strides before having to make any decision

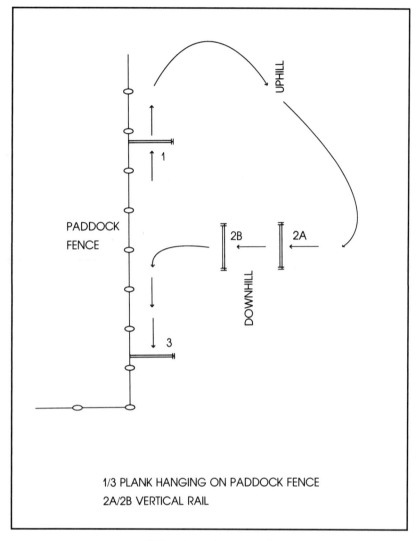

PADDOCK
FENCE

UPHILL

DOWNHILL

1

2B   2A

3

1/3 PLANK HANGING ON PADDOCK FENCE
2A/2B VERTICAL RAIL

Using terrain to teach

at all. Even though this exercise greatly improves the rider's sense of knowing where she is, when Mike asks her for an opinion of how it went, he gets a complicated response covering everything from the horse's right shoulder to the rider's left heel. It becomes clear to him that this is a rider with too much on her mind. He seeks to simplify it for her.

Sticking with the line they did in eight strides, Mike now asks her for the same thing in nine strides. The rider asks, "Do I put the extra

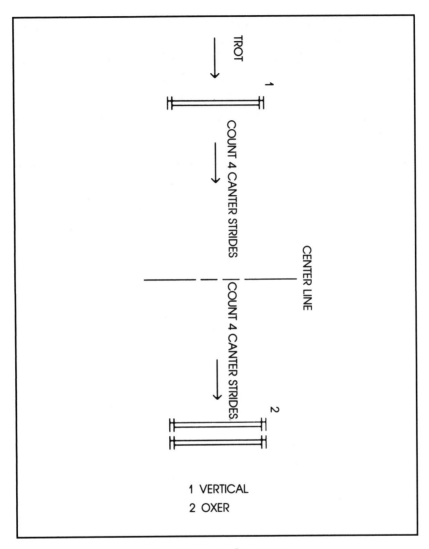

TROT

1

COUNT 4 CANTER STRIDES

CENTER LINE

COUNT 4 CANTER STRIDES

2

1 VERTICAL

2 OXER

Breaking up the count

stride in my first group of strides or my second group?" Mike again assures her there is no absolute answer. "Anyway you want. Experiment. Remember, there is no wrong . . . there is just learning."

Back and forth they go, doing the line in seven strides or eight strides or nine strides until the rider is able to recognize when she has to adjust to make the strides work. "You have the ability to lengthen and shorten the stride at your wish. Don't be afraid of it not working. If it doesn't work, you'll learn something about your horse." The more she practices, the better she gets at making the second jump happen.

As a final test of her growing skill, Mike asks her to ride a six-stride line on the diagonal to the seven-stride line on the outside. The lines ride very differently, the first is a going line and the second line is steady. "Create the horse that makes the job easy," Mike advises, nudging her towards considering the different rides she will need to make each line look professional. "Do the first line in two groups of three

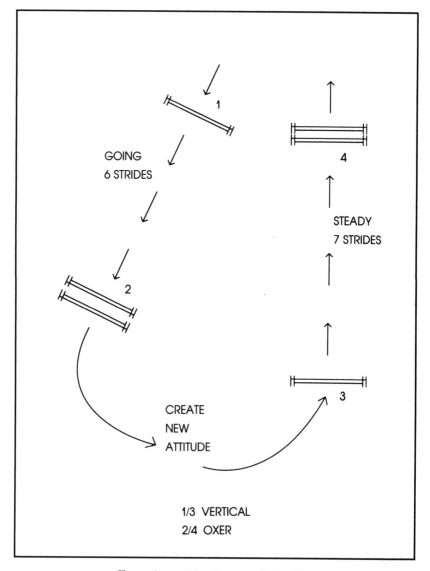

Changing attitude to suit the line

strides. Relax for the first three and see where you are. Through the end of the ring, create the new horse you need for the steady seven. He can't come to the second line with the same attitude he had at the first. Create a new horse, a horse with a little shorter stride keeping the rhythm. By changing your horse's body, adding a short release over jump 3, and adding a soft 'whoa,' you've told your horse repeatedly that the second line is different from the first."

The rider starts with a circle showing a short canter. Mike has her circle until she can get the stride longer. "Create what you need in the opening circle, not at the jump and not at the distance." She works out the exercise and does it well. Mike comments that most people who worry about finding the second jump do better when they break the strides into two groups. Not only does the horse benefit, but it helps riders who can't recognize a distance push their eye and train it. "You'd be surprised how you can push a rider's eye by breaking up the strides. They gain confidence as they are able to form mental pictures of how many strides there are between jumps."

With the successful completion of this exercise, teacher and student discuss her problems. "You worry about too many things. You are trying to worry about ten things when you can only remember maybe five. You've given yourself an impossible task. You can train like mad in the schooling area and worry about the details there, but once you walk into the ring to compete, you must go back to the most basic of principles. It makes no difference whether you are riding into the Grand Prix ring or a three-foot hunter warmup. You have to go straight. You have to go forward. You have to find the jumps. That is all you have to do."

Mike goes on to explain that if the horse does something on course you don't like, you fix it in the schooling area. The only things to worry about in the show ring are the particular problems the course presents. He says when you enter the show ring, "You don't worry about what your horse does. You don't worry about your horse's response to the jumps. You go into the ring with the belief that your mount will be perfect and his responses to you will be perfect." After that, it is up to previous training and rider instinct to make little corrections as needed. "Keep it simple in your mind. If your horse is going too fast, just think slow down, not a lot of complicated ways to slow down, just think slow down. Keep it simple, so your mind is free to analyze the problems created by the course."

According to Mike the show ring is not the place for the rider to try complicated maneuvers. Neither can the horse absorb them in a show ring situation where there is just too much distraction. Mike advises using the pre-ring warmup as a time to test mechanisms, tune in on the weaknesses and then forget it all. "You have a list of priorities when you go in the ring. First, you must establish the correct rhythm for the length of the line. Then you must create the line in your eye. Thirdly, you look for a distance and finally, you jump. All of these build on one another. They don't replace each other. You see, the distance is not the number one priority (although many novice riders think it is). Distance is created by rhythm and line. Once you have those, ninety-nine-percent of the time, the distance will be brought to you." Mike says what you don't do is go into a ring, pick up any pace on any line while you are staring at the jump telling yourself, "I've got to find a distance!" You'll never find one that way, he says assuredly.

In all our examples, Mike showed how the exercise does much of the teaching. His skilled and colorful way of imparting information goes a long way toward making the student receptive to learning and confident when performing.

❑ *Clinic information can be obtained by contacting Mike Henaghan at Newstead Farm, P.O. Box 219, Upperville, VA 22176; 703-592-3636.*

DANA JUNGHERR

"Right from the start, teach children the correct flat work."

James Leslie Parker

AFTER GRADUATION FROM HER VERY SUCCESSFUL JUNIOR YEARS WITH VICTOR HUGO VIDAL, DANA TOOK OVER CEDAR LODGE IN CONNECTICUT. THERE SHE TRAINED MANY EQUITATION FINALISTS AND RIBBON WINNERS—ELIZABETH FRENCH, MARTHA FULTON, SUSIE SCHROER, TO NAME A TRIO. EIGHT YEARS IN MASSACHUSETTS FOLLOWED, WHERE SHE AGAIN TRAINED TOP JUNIOR RIDERS AND DEVELOPED EQUALLY FAMOUS HORSES, SUCH AS LITTLE BIG MAN, FLAMINGO AND MAGIC DRAGON. CURRENTLY, DANA TRAINS AT ACRES WILD FARM IN RHODE ISLAND WITH PAUL VALLIERE WHERE THEY TURN OUT MANY OF THE TOP JUNIOR RIDERS OF THE DAY.

The Flat

Dana works a great deal with the young riders at Acres Wild. She feels strongly that it is never too early to teach children how to ride. "Right from the start I like to teach my kids, even if they are on ponies, as I would teach the older students. You have to treat them like they're young because they are. You have to remember that mentally it's a little bit harder for them. But you really have to teach them, from the start, the proper flat work." Her lessons reflect the fact that she is developing future equitation and jumper riders. I found Dana's patience and levelness with her students to be admirable and I found she teaches her youngest riders to think and feel rather than mimic.

Today's lesson is with an eleven-year-old rider mounted on a medium pony. It is a successful pony but not always an easy ride. The student starts with a posting trot as Dana reminds her they are building on the last lesson. "Now, think about what we've been working on: keeping a straight line from the bit to your hand to your elbow. Carry your hands a little bit off your pony's neck—not burying your pinkie in your pony's wither. You are really stretching deep in your heel, trying to keep your base of support underneath you. Your hip angle is a little closed in the post trot and your back is hollow with your shoulders back." Dana's use of words such as "you are" instead of "you should" is a vital element of her success in communicating with her youngest students. She doesn't stint on the praise when the rider finds just the right balance and shape.

"Because you are trotting around to your pony's stiffer side, let's put him a little more on the inside bend and think about your pony's weight moving from your inside leg to your outside direct rein. You are always pushing him out in the turn and balancing him with your outside rein. That's your most important rein. You don't want to ride on the inside rein."

Dana's manner makes the difficulty of the flat work seem routine. She uses simple words to explain hard concepts. "Come down the center line and let's change your direction. Now you're straight and then you put him slightly on the new bend before you make the turn. As you bend him right, support him with your right leg so he doesn't fall in. Don't let your reins get too long."

One step ahead of the rider, Dana is able to control and guide the student for maximum results. "Now think about pushing him off the inside leg, balancing him to the outside rein." In her effort to get more bend from the pony, the student crosses her inside rein over the horse's wither to the outside. "Don't ever take the inside rein and cross it over his neck. You never cross the rein over, okay? Carry a shorter rein, and you can use your slight indirect inside rein without having to cross the neck. If you find your hands over your thighs, you know your reins are too long."

As the rider is circling and attempting to bend the pony she has started to tip her body toward the inside. "As you push him with the right leg, don't lean right and dip down with the shoulder. I don't want

Cannell

Student Erica Keany demonstrates correct arm position.

to see what you do from the waist down in your upper body." Dana notes that we need to teach young riders that from the waist up they should bend in the direction the pony is traveling and yet stay in the center of their horse.

"Come back up the center line, seeing the corner of his eye and the corner of his nose as he comes through the turn, then go straight. Then put him slightly on the left bend before the turn. Feel the right rein and keep your left leg so he doesn't cut in. Act as if somebody is pulling your head to the sky so you stretch up tall while you are sinking deep into your heel."

We are back to circling on the pony's stiffer side. The student feels the difference right away and resorts to stronger use of her hand to keep him out on the curve. "You need to push him with your left thigh, your left calf, to the outside rein. Don't hang on that indirect rein, you'll just get him to hang harder on the inside."

Dana asks the rider to go to the collected sitting trot, which she notes, is not the favorite gait of ponies or young children. "Feel his mouth directly . . . bend your elbows . . . and slow him down. Steady him on the outside rein. Act like you weigh two hundred pounds and sit in the saddle heavy. Hands apart . . ." Noting the propensity for pony riders to keep their hands close together because it makes them feel safer, Dana asks her rider to separate her hands four to five inches apart, "So you have a right side and a left side."

Another change of direction is asked for. With the change, the rider leans forward. "Bring his mouth to you. Don't get stuck leaning up your pony's neck. Hold your body position. The strength of your position is in the small of your back. Half-halt him by pushing him from your seat and leg to your hand and bring his mouth to you. Now show the collected posting trot, remembering to bend your arm at the elbow, not allowing your arms to get straight." Dana says it's important to keep a watchful eye on the length of stirrups with young riders. You want them long enough so the rider learns to reach down in the thigh and yet short enough so that the knee angle isn't compromised by the leg getting too straight. Because children grow so quickly, it is likely their stirrup lengths will need adjustment fairly frequently.

The student is asked to show a two-point position. Dana tells me this rider has a tendency to let her lower leg slip back in the half-seat, which tips her upper body forward over the top of the jumps. Dana explains how this affects her performance. "Then she can't land into her base of support ready to ride to the next jump." Exaggeration and repetition are two tools Dana uses to get her point across to children. "Because of her habit, I'm going to ask her to almost kick her leg out in front of her. When it starts to really get in front of her, we'll change it."

"Hold that position and change direction. Remember the elbow. Stay in this position and increase the trot." The two-point, or half-seat position is a favorite of Dana's. She tells me she uses it a great deal because it is so good for getting young riders deep into their legs and heels while keeping the proper position for the leg. "Eventually, I make the kids work for hours without stirrups, but at this age I don't ask for quite as much."

Dana wants to see young riders forming good, solid positions so they can learn to work their horses properly. A rail on the ground is added to the exercise. The rider is directed to keep a medium posting trot over the pole and then show an increase in the trot after the rail. After the rail, she is to execute a circle where she will slow the trot again. Not surprisingly, as soon as an obstacle is introduced, the obstacle takes over the rider's concentration. By asking for pace changes, Dana is forcing her pupil to think about her flat work even though she is excited by the cavalletti.

"You've got to keep your mind and your eyes ahead of you. As you collect him, remember that everything you do is always: seat, leg, then hand. You're pushing from your seat and leg up into your hand, where you resist him to shorten the stride. If you want to lengthen him, you do the same with your seat and leg, but your hand allows him to go forward with a feel on the reins. Never open your fingers. Soft is not open fingers . . . it's feel and give through the arm and the elbow."

The rider is asked to add a flower-box jump to the exercise. "Slow the trot down, more than what you have." Pony riders often rely on their hands for upper body balance, and many of them depend on their hands exclusively to steer. The result is a pony stiff to the bit and stiff through the neck. "No. Don't pull down to slow him. Instead, feel his mouth directly towards your waist and push him with your leg. Make a small circle . . . pushing him out through the turn with your inside leg at the girth and keep your outside leg just a little back to prevent him from moving his haunches out on the turn. Don't keep shortening on that inside rein to make a turn. Use your seat and leg to turn him."

The rider goes back to the collected sitting trot, demonstrating an exaggerated bend. "Don't lean over your hands as you work them. Sit on your seat bones a little bit and look at me . . . feeling his mouth." The rider changes direction. "Left lead canter now. Don't lean for the canter depart, instead, sit a little bit on the outside seat bone, using the outside leg and inside rein. He's not really cantering there, so you need more seat and leg while you keep a light feel of his mouth, so you can think about shaping him."

Dana uses cavalletti and brush boxes as exercises to train the young rider's eye without wearing out the pony. This youngster canters the pole and turns to canter the flower box. With repetition of the exercise, both pony and rider get bolder making the distances over the fences long and weak. "Find the center of the jumps, shorten him while creating impulsion from your seat and leg. Put him deep to the jumps. Use more leg—always use the leg to shorten. After the pole, let's see an increase in canter to the box. Ride up to it and make it happen. Short stride to the pole and then show me a lengthening to the box." The rider accomplishes this task quickly, since it is an extension of all the work she has done this lesson. She reverses and repeats the exercise. This time the lengthening to the flower box will require more concentration because the box is directly away from the ingate.

Dana moves on to teaching the rider adaptability. She wants her student to be able to use both her two-point and her three-point positions. First, she has the rider show a two-point on a circle, reminding her to keep her arms bent while out of the saddle and to use her leg to keep the pony out on the circle. The rider is then asked to connect her seat and increase the pace of the canter. "You are going to make him go forward in the full-seat position with your hands apart and your fingers closed around the reins. Now I want to see you collect the canter. Before you half-halt him, show me a deep seat; push him with your seat and leg to your hand."

"Show me a half-turn with a flying change of lead. Remembering not to lean." The rider is caught at the change, relying too much on the inside rein rather than using her inside leg to push the pony out. This causes a late change behind. "If he's hanging on your left hand, don't hang back. That's not going to lighten him. You need to keep working on your left leg, balancing him out to your right rein."

Dana asks for an increase in canter pace again. The canter remains pretty much the same speed, and she reminds her rider, "Make sure when you tell him to do something, you don't just expect him to do it. You tell him and then you are aware of getting your results or not. Be aware. Make sure what is happening is what you are asking for."

Back at the collected canter on the left lead, the rider is asked to canter the two jumps again. Her pony has a tendency to jump the right corner of his jumps and land on the right lead more often than not. Dana gives the rider a correction to deal with the problem. "Keep him a little bit on the left bend at the top of the jump, and keep your outside leg to hold him on the lead. It's just like holding him on the circle . . . think about it."

Dana adds downward transitions to the exercise as a way of reminding the rider to use her seat and leg to get compliance from the pony. "When you come from a canter to a trot, get him collected first and then you can ask him to move ahead. And halt. Make him stand. You ride the downward transition by sitting. Push him from your seat and leg and feel his mouth, getting him to step up underneath as he comes down to the halt so he stays in a shape." The rider repeats the canter-halt transitions until she learns not to lean forward with her upper body to accomplish it.

Dana notes that many pony riders ride with too long a rein, and she says she frequently knots the reins to teach the students to carry their hands in front of them.

Our student has changed direction, demonstrating a flying lead change. She canters the flower boxes and comes back to a collected sitting trot. "Drop your stirrups, just for a minute, and show me a posting trot without them. Keep your leg a little long." Dana explains that because the rider is young she won't ask her to work without irons for a long time, but will ask her to do it often for short periods of time. This way she builds strength and position gradually.

A change of direction allows Dana to check the position of both legs without stirrups. "Now, decrease the trot, with both reins, and let's sit the trot. Now, find your stirrups without looking for them, and go to the posting trot, lengthening his trot while keeping his shape. Pretend it's a hack class—show him off."

While our rider rests, Dana talks about the pony riders who have trouble getting their legs around wide-bodied ponies. "If they step a little heavy on the inside of their foot and break their ankle a little inward and downward, the leg seems to fall into the proper place without wiggling."

Jumping

Dana sets up a small gate on the diagonal for the rider to use as a warmup. She admits this is an unusual first jump for this student. She allows the jump to be trotted toward home the first time, to give the pony and student extra confidence.

"Make a circle first and think about it. He hasn't jumped in a few days. You want to be solid with your leg and spell it out for him; you are going to trot that jump." The student has no problem with this first exercise. She is asked to canter the jump, which she does with a chip in. "He went to stall out in front of that jump, didn't he? I don't think

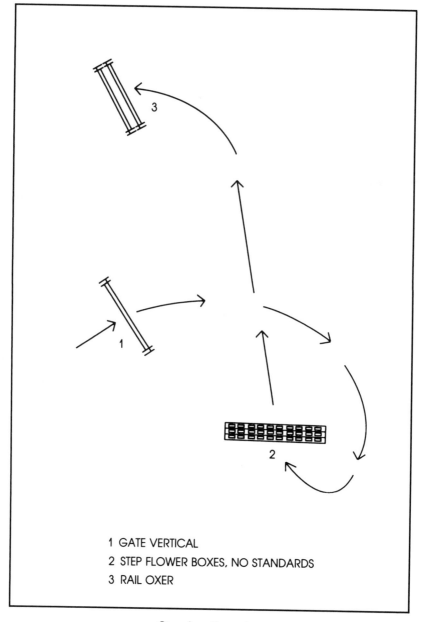

1 GATE VERTICAL
2 STEP FLOWER BOXES, NO STANDARDS
3 RAIL OXER

Steering Exercise

he knows what you want. If you feel that stall, you need to add a little bit of a cluck. Try to prevent it from happening rather than reacting after it happens." Dana raises the gate, adding the two-point and three-point positions already practiced on the flat to the exercise. "There are times to be in the half-seat and times to be in the full seat. You can connect your seat with the saddle as you get closer to the jump so he doesn't think he can get there and let you down."

Dana says she instructs her young riders to connect their seats for collection, lead changes, peeky ponies or for just slowing down. "I have them connect their seats until they've accomplished what they wanted and then have them change back to the two-point."

The next exercise is harder. The student is told to canter the gate and roll around a tight turn to jump a pile of gray boxes that are loaded with bright and potentially spooky flowers. This little jump has no standards to direct the pony toward the middle. Following that, the rider is to make a left bending turn to an oxer on the diagonal, headed toward the outgate. This is performed beautifully as the rider concentrates on the job she wants the pony to do.

Dana adds a jump that both she and the rider know the pony doesn't like. A gray wall oxer off a short right-hand turn. Following the right-hand landing she is to ride down the ring a bit and make a shorter right-hand turn to a box oxer. "We practice a lot of turns with the kids to teach them how to use their seats and legs and how to be accurate. We teach them to come around the turns and straighten out of the turns. It's hard to find a distance to the jump if you don't have your pony or horse straight. If their [the animal's] shoulders are to the left, or their hips to the right, for example, and you go to move up, it won't happen. If you want to wait, your horse will move to the side."

Many pony riders zing around a course with the wind pushing pigtails into a contrail behind them. I asked Dana how she teaches pace to her young riders. "We work on a lot of turns and circles, and that is the time we teach them collection. There are always regrouping periods on the course, so after they jump a line, they land and regroup. It enables them to get the pony back so they can ride up to the pace needed for the next jump. If they keep going fast, fast, faster, pretty soon they won't be able to find the jumps from that pace; they'll get really long or start chipping in. So I always tell them to ride up . . . and then regroup. They learn to do this so well—to wait mentally and

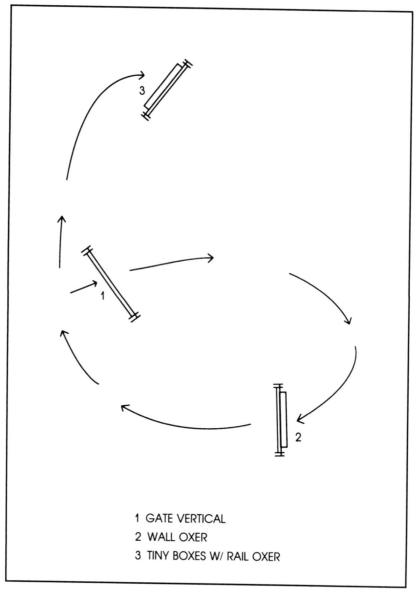

1 GATE VERTICAL
2 WALL OXER
3 TINY BOXES W/ RAIL OXER

Connecting Exercise

physically before riding up—that it's invisible. The pace becomes even and smooth and the jumps turn out the same."

Dana says they also practice lots of lines doing optional strides so the rider can start relating pace to strides too. "It's good to have a mix of turns and straight lines so the kids learn to steer, collect, go forward or steady a line." She feels too many pony riders do not practice turns as often as lines.

It has become busy around the jumps we are using for this lesson, and the rider has not only to execute the course properly, but also keep an eye out for oncoming traffic. Dana gives her a course of a long approach to a single jump, to a right turn going to a straight line, to a bending line. She discusses the potential trouble spots with her rider before she begins jumping. "Connect your seat after the straight line; he might look at the jump since he's only jumped it the other way. Don't let him get too slow, because when he gets behind your leg he wobbles left and right. Be there with your seat and legs. Think about what you're doing."

The exercise is done well the first time, although the pony got behind her leg when he was distracted by all the activity. "You need to get going on your opening circle. The circle is where you prepare for your course." Dana gives the rider a new course which involves more turning and a spooky log jump. This will reinforce the need for the rider to connect her seat. She will jump the same first fence, make a right-hand turn to an oxer and then a right-hand turn to the log jump. "This pony likes to slow down to the jumps, so remember your seat. Get more pace to keep him straight. Make your rollback to the log through the middle but remember he doesn't like it, so go past it just a bit and steer back with your leg, so he has lots of time to see it. Ride up to that jump with your eye up." Then she is told to turn left and jump the rolltop in a straight line to the gate. After that, a hard right hand turn to the flower boxes, a right again to the oxer. After the oxer she'll show a halt, making him stand before backing up, finally, she'll trot out over the vertical. "If you let him drift right over the gate you'll get to the flowers too early, so connect your seat and ride him out a bit. When you back him up after the halt, you know he's going to want to swing his hips to the left, so use your left leg when you back up."

It starts out too slowly. "Be there, make it happen, give him a kick if you need it. Make him pay attention. Look up and don't pull down." The rider executes the test very well with the exception of getting long to the final oxer, which made her halt rough. Like many pony riders, she closes her hip angle too much and lies on the pony's neck in the air. Dana warns that this is one of the worst habits pony riders develop

Erica Keany in competition

as they grow. They have no place to put their bodies, so they end up ducking off to the side. The rider is sent back to find a smaller distance to the oxer and instructed to keep her hip angle open to facilitate the halt.

This very young rider has practiced some fairly advanced techniques and has been able to see the relationship between her position and the jumping effort she gets from her pony. She has been asked to jump an obstacle with no standards, to get lead changes, to change her seat, to regulate her pace and to look up. She has been exposed to a more advanced vocabulary and is learning the essence of more difficult techniques. Dana says, "It's not the height they need to practice—it's the precision they need to learn." This kind of riding will make the big step up to the junior hunter and equitation classes much easier.

❏ *Clinic information can be obtained by contacting Acres Wild, 260 Pound Hill Road, North Smithfield, RI 02895; 401-766-1051.*

TIM KEES

*"Eye is the most important and
least used of our natural aids."*

Cannell

WALTER "TIM" KEES, JR., IS THE SON OF A
RIDING FATHER WHO WAS CONSIDERED
A STYLIST BEFORE WE EVEN PLACED A
VALUE ON THE WORD IN REGARD TO RID-
ING. HIS MOTHER WAS THE LEADING
WOMAN TRAINER OF RACEHORSES IN
AMERICA AS TIM GREW UP. ALTHOUGH
HORSEMANSHIP WAS ALWAYS A BIG
PART OF HIS LIFE, HE DIDN'T PICK UP THE
TRAINING OF JUNIOR RIDERS UNTIL RON-
NIE MUTCH ASKED HIM TO BE A PART OF
NIMROD FARM IN CONNECTICUT. SINCE THAT TIME TIM'S STUDENTS HAVE CONSISTENTLY PLACED
AND OFTEN WON THE EQUITATION FINALS. UNDER THE NORFIELD FARM NAME, TIM HAD CON-
TINUED SUCCESS WITH HIS HORSES TOO. HOLY SMOKE, KILLER TOM, WATERSHIP DOWN, FANTAS-
TICO AND OTHERS WORE THE BEIGE AND BLUE COLORS OF THE FARM. TODAY, TIM IS PARTNERED
WITH JEFFREY WELLES, TURNING OUT MANY WINNERS IN NEW YORK. TIM HAS AN UNUSUAL VERBAL
STYLE THAT IS A TRADEMARK OF THIS WINNING TRAINER.

The Flat

Tim was most generous in allowing me to watch lessons, and what
follows is a composite of the three students I observed. Each lesson
began with walk-trot transitions. "Start with a brisk medium
trot . . . relaxing your arm to get him in front of you." The student is
working on a large left-handed circle around Tim. "Think left leg and
a little right rein. Keep him very, very straight. Lift your chest a little

bit and think in terms of relaxing your arm so he's out in front of your leg. By always pitching yourself a little forward, he's always going to be running forward." This rider has a tendency to tip forward to her post to start her horse up. Tim explains that if she stays pitched forward, it will show up at the jumps, with the horse always running forward in an effort to get underneath the rider's body. "Back to the walk, making sure your hip comes underneath of you and raise your chest so your horse comes in front of your leg. Your eye is forward, making it infinitive that he keeps following your eye. You keep straightening and forcing him to the track your eye creates—which is forward. Your eye only operates on a straight line. You want to get to where you're looking." Tim has the rider post the trot before walking again. "Keep adding at the walk. Be more definitive when you sit. You should be sitting deep and to the front of the saddle. Let him know where you are so he doesn't have to keep shifting to get his body underneath of you."

Tim is constantly explaining to his students how their riding affects the balance of the horse. He wants the rider to understand how to influence performance rather than just go along for the ride. "Posting trot, lift your chest, feel his right side. You are ahead of him. Can you feel him get dull in your hand? You can actually do a sitting trot for a few steps until you feel him out in front of your leg." The horse is occasionally tripping behind, and Tim sees that as a weakness on the part of the rider. "When you feel him buckling or tripping there, it's because his hip is displaced to the inside. Add a little more left leg there to correct that. You want to keep his hip straighter. Go back to your walk . . . keep adding and remind him to stay in front of you and stay active. Posting trot . . . really stretch up and relax your hands as you let him step into the transition. You can flex him using both hands to the right with a little left leg to watch that hip." They practice a few more transitions, with Tim encouraging the rider to execute them correctly with both her aids and her body position, thus enabling the horse to "step up" into the downward and upward transitions. Tim reminds his student, "It is always leg to hand." Tim points out that her horse isn't cleanly stepping up into his transitions because he is always displacing his hip left before he goes straight. Immediate response is vital for equitation riders, so they continue to work on correcting the horse's evasion. "Usually the best way to get a horse to be straight is to go forward, but remember a horse can only open or close his stride if he is straight. It is the only way you get true steps, be them up, be them down."

Tim has the rider change direction and tells her to carefully monitor her horse's hip position, keeping him very straight through the turn. "Don't lose his hip there...feel him with your left leg." The horse raises his head with the change of direction and Tim gives the correction: "Always follow the resistance...as he raises up, follow it...fix your hand, but keep straightening and driving from your leg to your

Kym Ketcham

The effect of uneven reins on a rider's position

103

hand because this is uncomfortable for him. The rider goes back to the posting trot, and because she tips forward with her first posting steps, the horse drops back. Tim asks her to work harder on her seat. He suggests that she sit into the brighter pace of the posting trot before she rises with the motion. "Establish where your seat is by sitting first. Think of a little haunches-in; both hands to the left and a little left leg back." The rider has let one rein slip through her hand so that the reins are uneven in length. "If you have one rein longer than the other, as your body seeks to establish contact, you will open your hip on the long-rein side. That forces you into a crooked position that sends mixed messages to your horse concerning balance." An uneven hip can cause a horse to drift or twist and can eventually lead to lameness on one side of the animal.

As the rider uses her leg to move her horse forward, he skips a step behind. Tim notices immediately, "That little skip means he is behind your leg. Put your left leg back. Now, straighten him and flex him in again making a half turn, keeping him very straight with your leg and your hand." The rider performs another half turn as Tim watches carefully. "Let him turn underneath of you, taking care you don't lose his haunch. Keep more weight in your heel so you don't pitch forward."

At the sitting trot, Tim asks the rider to show a shoulder-in. "Keep both hands a little to the right and keep your right leg back. Pick up your right lead [canter]." Tim notes that the shoulder-in is a preface to the right lead on this circle. Canter-sit trot transitions work on the joint problems of a lazy horse and an indefinite ride. "Get going—don't let it be dull. Now slow down going back to the sitting trot, flex him in and follow. The follow is his reward. Boxing the stride is the discipline, relaxing the stride, that's the reward."

As they work on getting the haunch alive through transitions, the horse tries a new evasion and cocks his head. "In order to cock his head, he has to cock his shoulder. Do another shoulder-in, then pick up your right lead. Giving and taking on the same plane—don't lower your hands." Tim has the student make a half-turn to the right holding the counter lead, followed by a half-turn back to the right circle, where she is encouraged to allow the horse to go forward as he is now carrying himself. The same exercise is repeated in the other direction. "You want his shoulders and hips on the same track. When you feel one side start to raise up, just take that side by following the resistance with a fixed hand and a stronger leg. Pick up the tempo. Don't let him fall behind your leg. When he slows down, you want to think in terms of lower miles per hour but higher rpms [revolutions per minute] behind." Tim tells me that the top equitation horses have to be able to step forward or melt back in a heartbeat, especially in the test situations. He slaps his hands together sharply to indicate how quickly they must be able "melt and stay alive." Tim is convinced that this rider does feel her horse fall behind her leg, but he feels her reaction to it isn't nearly quick enough.

Kym Ketcham

Demonstrating the counter canter

Jumping

Tim has his students warm up over a small vertical that is part of a two-stride combination. They are to jump it on the angle. They begin at the canter, disciplining themselves to hold the line.

After cantering the jump a couple of times, Tim asks the riders to make a figure eight out of the one jump. Once the horses are warmed

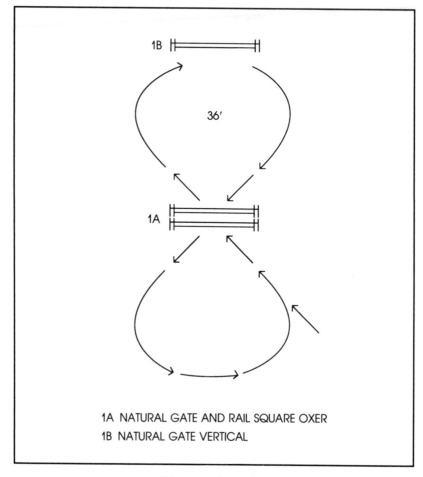

1A NATURAL GATE AND RAIL SQUARE OXER
1B NATURAL GATE VERTICAL

Warmup Exercise

up and the riders have been able to hold the line well, they are asked to continue the pattern, but this time they are to trot the first jump and canter the second. "This energizes the horse's back end," Tim explains. Now Tim changes the exercise to just jumping the oxer (the second part of the two stride) on the angle to practice eye discipline and line maintenance.

Next he asks the riders to get the two-stride twice, once in each direction. One student stands off to a long, weak distance. "By leaning forward to find the distance you forced the horse to fall behind you. In that situation you are either going to be lucky or unlucky. Fix it by keeping your horse in front of your leg."

Tim explains this rider needs her work to be geared toward understanding miles per hour (mph) and revolutions per minute (rpm) so she can learn to understand and appreciate different distances. "Without the hind end alive, you give yourself no choices," he warns.

The riders are given an exercise of the two-stride to a wall panel jump on an angle. Going toward the barn, they are asked to get the six strides between the out and the panel. The six is a tight line. Following that, they are asked to return in the opposite direction, getting the five between the panel and the in-and-out. Cautions Tim, "The five is very loose." The exercise, showing control of stride, is accomplished easily.

The next exercise involves a liverpool jump in a triple combination. Water jumps often intimidate equitation horses and riders. To allow both horse and rider time to deal with it, Tim asks the riders to jump the liverpool as a single jump alone on a figure-eight pattern.

As soon as they have relaxed at this jump, the exercise increases in difficulty. Eye control will be all important. The riders are asked to jump the liverpool on an angle, then come back on it, go around the middle jump of the combination to the final oxer, which will also be ridden on the angle. "Be disciplined about your eye. Just guide them— don't break them up." Despite his warnings, one rider lets her horse shift off the line, which creates a long, scrambling jump. "Just guide him, feel him. Don't push yourself back in the saddle and then lean forward. That forces the horse to elongate his stride, making a long, flat or 'dead' stride."

At the level at which Tim's students compete, there is no doubt that the equitation tests separate the winners from the losers. That's not to say you don't have to be good enough in the first round to be called

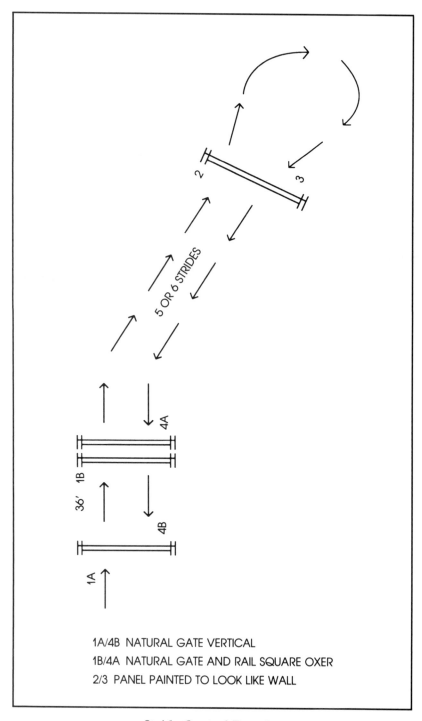

1A/4B NATURAL GATE VERTICAL
1B/4A NATURAL GATE AND RAIL SQUARE OXER
2/3 PANEL PAINTED TO LOOK LIKE WALL

Stride Control Exercise

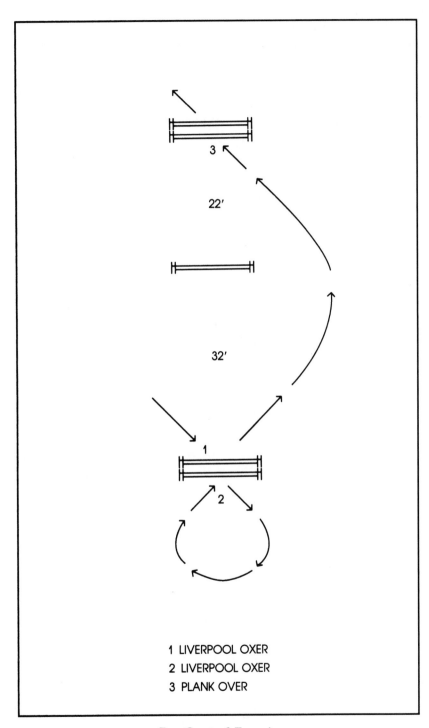

Eye Control Exercise

back for testing, but his students are seasoned competitors. They expect, and usually deliver, a strong first round. Because Tim's students are so strong on the tests, I asked him to include some in his lesson.

The first test we asked of the demonstrating rider was to trot a fence. "A trot jump is one of the few places you can actually slow down. You really want to slow down to the distance, keeping them very, very straight." He has his student trot back on it with a warning: "Keep in mind that when you look down and stand on your toe on landing, there is no contact with the horse's mouth. Trot the jump again and halt with your eye fixed forward."

Tim asks the rider to trot the jump, halt and show a left counter lead to a vertical. "Keep in mind that as you trot this jump your eye will automatically go off center right. Honor that, because that is the track, and the track is inside of you. You already know where to go. As long as your eye is forward, you instinctively know where to go. Don't let your horse go left even though that will be his reaction because the jump is off to his left. Keep him straight, don't let him bend himself or shift. He needs to land straight." Tim explains that the most important issue of the halt is that the horse be ready for the next effort. "That means making sure your eye is up, so they step up to the next obstacle from underneath you."

"Show the halt. Now pick up your left counter lead." The rider performs this test a little roughly. "Okay, we'll do it again. Now use voice off the ground. You need a bit of a tranquilizing effect so the horse just knows mentally that he doesn't need to land thinking forward. Have a fixed hand and add your leg with your eye forward so he stays up, out in front of you, and keeps his body on the line created by your eye. By using your voice off the ground he'll land more shallow and the halt will be completed more quickly and cleanly."

Tim explains that "position is a big deal" in testing. "What a lot of the kids do, because they get anxious about the distance is they tend to slide back [in the saddle]. That pitches them forward over the jump. Because they are not in balance with the horse, more effort is involved in clearing the obstacle, as the horse has to push harder to compensate. The rider has lost contact, so the horse lands way out [from the jump], making the halt late and sloppy."

I ask Tim to detail a walk jump. "To walk a jump you really need to get up to the jump. This is where position is a truly a big deal." Tim

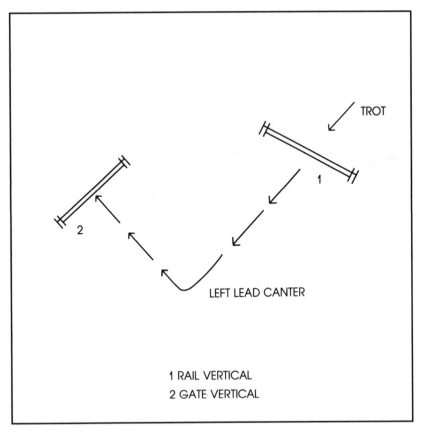

TROT

1

2

LEFT LEAD CANTER

1 RAIL VERTICAL
2 GATE VERTICAL

First Test: Trot fence 1, counter canter fence 2

explains that the horse has to be free to look down at a walk jump and gauge it. The goal is to have the horse stay up through his back but look down at the jump. "What happens to most juniors when they walk a jump is that they get very erect, so they are not following the horse's use of his head and neck." Tim says it's important to position the rider so that he/she is ready for the jump. The rider should be "Right in the front of the saddle, seated lightly, slightly closed [hip angle], with a raised chest," so the rider in no way interferes with the jump but enables the horse to gauge the jump without worrying. Tim asks our demonstrator to show me the correct rider position for various test requirements. She is instructed to walk the first jump, make a right turn to canter the vertical in the middle of the double, halt, show a right counter lead through the double, and trot the first jump backwards. Tim tells

Kym Ketcham

Showing perfect position to a trot jump

me that "Once the riders get good, they begin to understand how incredibly important their position is. If you slide back at all or you don't steer—steering is the thing—you won't succeed."

Our rider begins her test. The halt comes some distance after the vertical. Tim explains that the halt comes too late as a result of her line to the vertical. Because she rode across the jump on an angle, a greater flight was created during the jump. The horse had to jump with more effort to clear the obstacle. "The greater effort came from the bigger push the horse needed to handle the jump on the angle, and that power, when it hit the ground, was too much. You want the halt to happen maybe eight feet after a jump."

After her second effort, Tim tells her to halt much sooner by finding the line the vertical is on. He tells her she allowed her horse to drift over the in and that caused the horse to have to power the jump. In

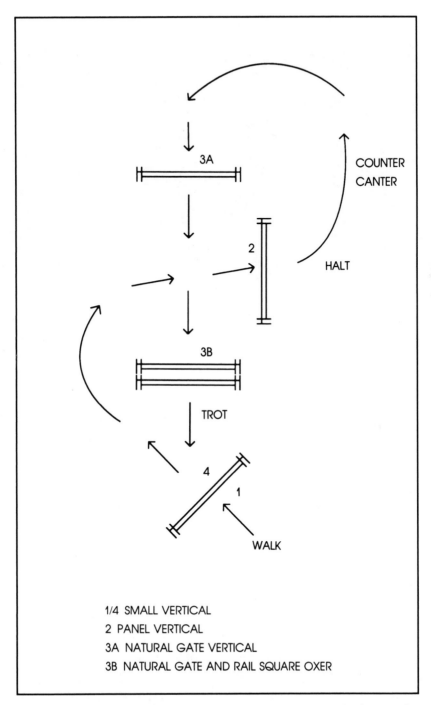

Second Test: Walk fence 1, canter 2, counter canter 3a/b, trot 4

Kym Ketcham

Demonstrating the greater flight caused by an angle jump

turn, that made the trot transition more difficult than it needed to be. "You should have your eye fixed on the trot jump even before you leave the ground for the double. Your eye is off center left there. Use your voice off the ground so that both of you are locked in to what you need to slow down for. The key is your eye. I want a very boxy distance . . . almost a haunches-in to the vertical for the dead distance."

The rider completes a clean halt a good twenty-five feet sooner than she had previously. However, she drops her eye at the halt and her horse backs up a step. "By looking down, you allow your horse to shut down and back up to you. Keep your eye forward, so your horse is ready to step up and forward into the next effort."

Tim asks the student to do one more test. "What you practice," he tells me, "is eye discipline. Not just teaching horses to halt, but how important the track is. The eye is the best tool we have and is, unfortunately, the least used."

The course is to canter fence 1, get a flying change (only if she needs it) to the counter lead to fence 2. Canter to fence 3. Halt. Counter canter to the vertical numbered 4. Tim tells his rider, "If your horse lands on the right lead after the first fence you will have to slow down, organize and get the change. Don't try for the change on an open stride. Make sure you jump the vertical as it is, not on an angle, before the halt. You want that to be an active, boxy distance and when you halt, feel the straightness but be looking at the last jump and you will instinctively know if you have enough horse to get up to the jump. By

Kym Ketcham

Horse and rider on track for the trot jump

looking at the last jump, your horse will lengthen or shorten his stride for the effort."

Tim explains that each of us has the ability to get from point A to point B built inside of us, just by looking ahead. What happens all too

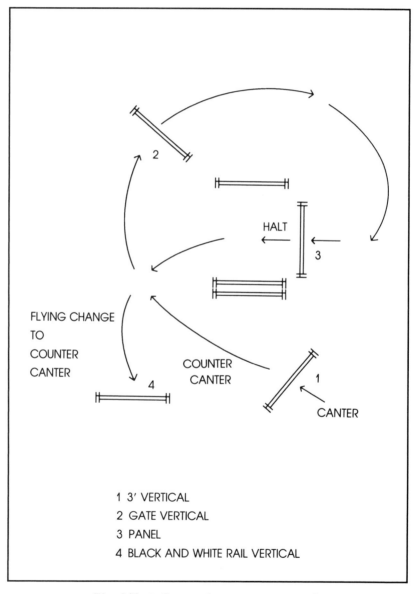

1 3' VERTICAL
2 GATE VERTICAL
3 PANEL
4 BLACK AND WHITE RAIL VERTICAL

Final Test: Canter 1, counter canter 2,
canter 3 and halt. Counter canter fence 4

Kym Ketcham

Student Hilary Bowers in the jumper ring

often is that a rider loses that line by not looking ahead at all times. In the test we are doing, Tim says many riders would be caught keeping their eyes on the line they had finished rather than on the line that is coming. By not using eye correctly, they would find their horse would have taken three or more strides before they were able to sight in on the next line.

In our exercise, the rider's first effort fails at the flying change to the counter lead. "Walk, pet him." Tim points out the teaching of testing takes time. He counsels patience. "If it doesn't happen the first time, relax, come back, and do it again. Take the time."

In the next effort the horse lands on the right lead and the rider tries to keep it. She is almost successful. "This is where the flat work is so important. Many people think you have to always keep a horse bent to the lead, but the truth is, you have to be able to ride a horse off of both reins. This is why we make them bend both ways when they counter canter. You can't become the sole proprietor of a distance by getting stuck with the outside bend in the counter canter. What if you have a big wide oxer to jump from the counter canter? Your horse has to be able to manage the effort of that jump."

The student is successful and rewarded with praise and a rest. "It's not only that a handful of trainers know testing; it's that the trainers who have had success in the finals understand how to teach the different tests. The key is the ability to understand your eye. Tim warns against too much testing work for the junior rider: "We don't torture the riders with testing. It can make your students regress. However, taken slowly, it's a building process."

❏ *Clinic information can be obtained by contacting Tim Kees, 24 North Combo, Westport, CT 06880; 203-454-9963.*

ANNE KURSINSKI

"Riding is about the horse and rider working together toward perfection."

Kym Ketcham

ANNE KURSINSKI IS THE MOST SUCCESS-FUL WOMAN RIDER THIS COUNTRY HAS EVER PRODUCED. IN A SHORTENED BI-OGRAPHY, SHE LISTS CREDITS SUCH AS THE TEAM AND INDIVIDUAL GOLD MEDAL WINNER IN THE 1983 PAN AM GAMES, THE TEAM SILVER AND INDIVIDUAL FOURTH PLACE IN THE 1988 OLYMPICS, THE 1991 L'ANNÉE HIPPIQUE LEADING LADY RIDER OF THE WORLD TITLE. IN 1991 SHE WAS THE WINNER OF THE GRAND PRIX OF AACHEN, CONSIDERED THE MOST PRESTIGIOUS GRAND PRIX IN THE WORLD. IN THE HISTORY OF THE EVENT, SHE WAS THE SECOND WOMAN TO EVER WIN AACHEN AND ONLY THE THIRD AMERICAN EVER TO DO SO. ADD TO THESE VICTORIES THE FACT THAT SHE WAS A UNITED STATES TEAM ALTERNATE FOR THE 1984 OLYMPICS AND THE 1988 AHSA HORSEWOMAN OF THE YEAR. SHE CONTINUES TO BE A CONSISTENT WINNER ON THE AMERICAN CIRCUIT AS WELL AS A SUCCESSFUL INTERNATIONAL COMPETITOR.

The Flat

Anne believes that good, basic dressage makes jumping easier. Flat work is a very important tenet of her teaching. It is her goal, when teaching, to help the rider become one with the horse. She tries to enable the rider to feel rather than perform on command. She feels strongly that a top rider isn't just a technician but rather a horseman, one who knows his/her horse in the stable as well as in the ring. She likes her riders to vary their riding experiences, mixing some cross country, pleasure hacking, and ring work, to make for well-rounded and refreshed competitors. She thinks too many of today's junior riders are both blessed and cursed by being good technicians. The plus side is that they can ride a more challenging course than in previous years; the negative side is that they can do so only with the advice of a trainer. She feels that many have sacrificed horsemanship for blue ribbons and have, along the way, lost the feeling—the feeling that makes a world class competitor and horseman. Riding should not just be about winning a class; it should be about the combination of horse and rider working together toward perfection. Anne is at the forefront of the mental approach to riding, using visualization to get results.

Our lesson this day is with one very advanced junior mounted on a green, slightly hot horse and a less experienced rider who is seeking to learn more than side, diagonal, side. The latter is not as well versed in the flat work as her fellow student, but is reaching to learn more.

Working in a lovely field, bordered with white fence, spotted with palm trees, the students begin at the working walk. "A much livelier walk, we are trying to make the horses more athletic. Keep your hands just above the withers. Your inside leg should be at the girth and your outside leg just a little back so you are bending your horse around your leg. Your left leg is pushing him out to your right rein." One rider's circle is too big, the other too small. "I'm in the center. You have to use your eyes for your spacing and the shape of your circle— that's just using your brain." Both riders start the posting trot, with Anne cautioning on keeping the correct bend. "Keep steady on both reins, just bending them no more than the circumference of the circle we are on." She asks both riders to walk and puts the less experienced rider behind the more advanced. "You watch, you're going to do a right leg-yield toward the fence. You keep him as straight as you can, trying to round him off a little in front. As you ride him sideways, you make him round in front. You'll notice that when you use your leg [to displace the haunch] he comes into the bit. That's leg to hand; that gives you the shape." She works both riders on this exercise twice more to reinforce riding both ends of the horse. "You've got to keep the horse perfectly straight, keeping the whole horse. You've got to ride the front of the horse, the back of the horse, and both sides of the horse." One of the horses decides to take exception to the leg pressure and shows his resistance by going sideways too much. "Forward, forward. When he starts getting silly, you've got to think forward." The other horse lies behind the command and Anne urges the rider to be more active in getting the haunches over. "You've got to listen to your horse, you've got to feel him. Keep the left rein, being active, active with your leg. You want to feel he uses his back and goes into the bit. You all have to learn to ride with your seat and your legs more." Anne notes that the riders must learn to make their horses better athletes, which she says is done by "listening to them, feeling them, understanding them."

The riders change direction at the walk to repeat the exercise in the other direction. They are asked for a left leg-yield out to the right. As with all horses, the change of direction means a change to the horse's other side, which may or may not be as strong. The gray horse falls behind his rider again. "Perfectly straight and into the bit. Don't be afraid to cluck a little and get him in front of you. He doesn't go into the bit because he's not honestly in front of the leg. Round him off in front as you move him over. In your mind, picture a round horse."

The posting trot is followed by a sitting trot. "Push him, make him use his back." The riders post down the far side of the pattern and return to the sit trot, showing the leg-yield in front of Anne. "You let his shoulder lead. He bends his head left and then pops his shoulder right. Leg him." The other horse is working up from the exercise. Anne counsels the rider to go straight until the horse settles: "Get the feeling he will relax in his withers as if you were doing long and low work. Think long and low. Tell him that. You're sitting down asking him to relax in his withers. Round but down. Legs, legs, legs, and ask him to stretch down. Reward him when he does it right. You have to be very clear with your aids."

The riders are told to do a half circle and repeat the exercise of posting trot on the far side and sitting trot with a leg-yield in front of Anne. "Picture what you want him to do . . . feel it, what you want him to do. You have to nicely tell him that [to do the leg-yield] and tell him the other [the evasion] is not allowed. When he's up like that you have to tell him, no, no, you've got to step under to come down. Keep sitting and get him to stretch down. Gently figure that out."

The less advanced rider is told to drop her stirrups, crossing them in front of her saddle, in order to teach her to better use her seat and legs to influence her horse. While she performs this task, the other student is still working with the greener horse. "The shape is important on this horse. The shape is more important than the actual leg-yield on this horse. Teach him that that's the only thing that's allowed. As your legs are asking for the lateral work, your arms are getting him to stretch. You've got to be able to do different things with different parts of your body." The horse is improving and the rider instructed to go to the posting trot, inviting him to stretch out more.

The younger rider is out on the circle at a sitting trot where she is working on getting the horse onto the bit. "You've got to feel the whole horse, ride the whole horse. I want him rounder. You know when you leg yield him it makes him rounder. We learned that. So make him rounder, feel his mouth, prick him with your spur, use a little cluck, without going faster. I want lots of impulsion that's packaged." At the walk this rider is asked to show a left leg yield to the right. "You get him connected, and you get the haunches . . . keeping your toes up." The horse is working on his stiffer direction and finds this maneuver difficult. "You've got to tell him what you want. Put your stick in your right hand, tap him behind your leg while you hold the shoulder. There, he is connected. Can you feel that? Don't lose it. Now move him back (a leg yield the other way) . . . keeping it active and round; prick him with your spurs—don't lose it. There's only one way to ride and that's the right way."

Anne has allowed the green horse to rest while she works with the gray, teaching the rider to get a round, active, obedient horse. The student goes back into the trot, losing some of the shape she'd managed to get at the walk. "Picture what you'd like him to look like. Keep the shape from your legs and seat . . . be active, active, active. Feel it." The pair succeeds and is allowed to rest. "If you are going to be a rider you have to work. You can't just sit there and pose. You want your horse to look totally different, to look like an athlete. If you just sit there, nothing happens."

The greener horse is still looking to get above the bit. "This upside down stuff has got to go away. You've got to be able to maintain shape; you can't rely on luck. You've got to teach him to be consistent and you have to be consistent. You have to become very steady. And that means not overcorrecting and not overrewarding. If you want him to stay there, then he should stay there. You have to figure that out. Nicely with your aids, you say to him, that's correct. If he goes too low, you have a little punishment; if he comes up too much, you have a little punishment. There, where you want him to be, it's very safe. But you have to be very, very consistent with your aids. You have to teach him to be steady."

At the posting trot the rider works on finding that fine line between correction and overreaction. "You have to be very, very sharp on this horse and really listening to your horse." At the sitting trot the horse shifts his haunches to the inside. Anne suggests the rider think of a shoulder-in as a correction. "It's like patting your head and rubbing your stomach. You need to be rounding him off in front and making him straight behind." At the posting trot they manage to keep better straightness and relaxation through the withers. At the sitting trot, he wants to hollow and get crooked. Anne has the student work on circles and changes in seat, from posting to sitting trot. "Don't overtrain, don't underdo it. Use lots of finesse." They continue to work through transitions in getting him to steady out and maintain carriage. "You have to ride him like this every single day; steady, steady, so he learns to do this to the jumps. The horse is an athlete and the rider is an athlete. This is not a beauty contest; pretty is as pretty does. When you ride well and the horse goes well, it's beautiful. We don't try to be beautiful. Beautiful is a result of your riding becoming an artwork. But first you have to work at it and the horses have to work at it." Anne compliments the rider on her advances in riding and notes that "Most people today don't listen to their horses and don't teach horsemanship. What makes a horse tick and why do they go a certain way and how can you change that."

Both riders are sent out to the rail with the less advanced rider behind the other for demonstration purposes. Anne asks for a right shoulder-in at the walk. "Both hands are going to shift a little bit to the right. Right leg at the girth. Both hands, by shifting to the right, will have the left rein against the neck to bring the shoulder to the right. Your right leg keeps the haunches on the imaginary straight line. You want to be slightly bent right with the shoulders about thirty degrees in from the track. You should see the corner of the right eye. Keep marching. Your diagonal aids: right leg, left rein are basically the main aids."

At the sitting trot, the riders are asked to show the shoulder-in on one side while keeping the horse's shape. One horse comes in off the track in response to the displacing leg. "He snuck way in off the track, didn't he? As you bring the shoulders in you've got to half-halt him so he doesn't run in. You have to not let the haunches come off the track.

That's your right leg." The more novice of the two riders is having trouble visualizing this exercise, confusing her aids with the leg yield. "Bring the shoulders toward me, with both hands slightly right. Don't get too much bend in the neck. If you bend the neck too much to the right you never get the shoulders over . . . they'll go left. Left neck rein and right leg, hard. Don't pull the neck in. As soon as you haul on the inside rein, the shoulder flies out." They work through the exercise until the rider is able to understand what she is asking the horse. Anne reminds the student that the head and neck of the horse are "only a reflection of what the back of the horse is doing. As soon as you get active with your leg and he gets active with his haunch, you get a beautiful shape."

A long rein walk to the other direction gives the horses a chance to rest. "All this flat work is like taking your horse to the gym and doing an aerobics class. It makes him a better athlete. It makes him stronger and straighter and honest to the aids. Then when you go to jump, the jumping should be easy. The jumps just get in the way."

Both riders work again on the shoulder in going in the new direction. They have to continue to work through the resistances of their individual horses. Anne warns that it is the rider's responsibility to make the horse equally strong on both sides.

The riders are asked to show a turn on the haunches: "Just swing the shoulders around." They are asked to relate this to the shoulder-in. "What are you doing? You are moving the shoulders [to the right]. That's exactly what you do in the shoulder in, where you just swing the shoulders in about a quarter of the turn, about thirty degrees. You can't do that if you are bending their heads toward the right." The less advanced student works on both the shoulder-in and the turn on the haunch so she can get the feel of swinging the front of the horse. "How do you move the front of the horse? How do you move the back of the horse? How do you move his neck? How do you make it go faster and slower?" Anne wants her students to understand the movements of the animal and how they relate to rider's aids.

After a breather, the riders are asked for a working canter to the left. She insists that the upward transition be clean, without any trot steps first. The green horse raises his head and neck and becomes crooked with the change of pace. "Almost ask him for a little bend to the right to keep him straight." This horse and rider combination works again on transitions; this time the trot-canter transition, to teach him to carry the steadiness he learned in the trot over to the canter work.

At the canter the riders are asked to show a right leg yield. "Don't let him increase his stride as you ask for the leg yield. He should be able to canter in place as he steps to the left. Just because you are using your leg doesn't mean he has to run away. Horses have to be between your hands and your legs. Legs create the impulsion and your hands package it.

"Most children don't have a clue how to move their horse. They don't have a clue how to feel the horse. People don't teach them how to ride the whole horse. Most teach them to ride the mouth, a few teach the legs, but very few teach the whole horse. The idea of using your hands and your legs and your back and your seats is foreign to many juniors." Anne believes that correct flat work makes the competitive horse. She also believes that a good flat program is vital in making a successful jumper. She asks her horses to work out strenuously on the flat, knowing that their knowledge of aids and shape will carry them over the jumps without the rider being forced to interfere with the jumping process.

Jumping

"Do it right the first time. You only have one chance to make a good first impression." In clinics, Anne mentions this fact often as she is faced with riders and horses both unknown to her and of checkered talents. She expects psychological toughness and physical softness from her riders. All of the work she does with students over fences is directed to get that result.

We have a large group lesson comprised of riders of all levels and all ages. There is no age limit when it comes to improvement. Each rider is reminded to work on the area of their known weakness while the more advanced are asked to think about the shape of the horse. On a figure eight, they are asked to trot in single file over a cavalletti. "This is a good time to work on your hands. The horse should go in self carriage." By working in a long line in single file, the riders have to be aware of each other in addition to themselves. Anne works with each rider's faults, from keeping heels down, to slowing down, to keeping the release low. "When you have rhythm and a good position you can add shape to it." The riders are directed to canter the cavalletti after it has been rolled up to a greater height. The more educated riders are encouraged to bend their horses in the air to land on the correct lead. Anne works toward getting the riders supple over this introductory exercise. She wants to see her riders demonstrating that "all your joints [are] hydraulic, so you can feel and follow the horse's mouth and motion."

One at a time, the riders are asked to trot down over a bright yellow and black box, which is a spooky first solo effort. "The biggest thing here is not to go too fast . . . the hands have to be low and together so the horse can't duck out. You have to be a little behind your horse even if you are leaning forward. You could be pushing a little with your seat. Your hands have to make sure they go straight. Hold your line with your eye, your hands and both seat bones."

Most of the horses pop over the box with only a slight peek. One junior rider has a harder time of it, as her horse spooks out to the side. "If you are going to be a rider, you have to ride. Get him right over that. You have to be smarter than your horse. You're weak. You should respond when you feel him moving out. It's not a beauty contest out here, you have to be a horseman. He's not going to do you any favors." Another rider has a problem that stems from not holding the line more than from a spook. As often happens with an uncertain jumping effort, a couple of the riders lose control of their arm motion. Anne reminds them that arm motion should be lateral only. Arms can go from side to side or forward and back but should never go up and down.

After all the students have successfully completed the exercise with confidence, they are asked to trot a vertical into a bending line. Anne wants a straight line done between the vertical and the next fence. They are to canter out of the line in five strides, counting each stride aloud. Following the second jump she wants to see a halt on the end of the line, "to get their mouths again."

A favored exercise when she holds clinics, Anne frequently has riders count aloud. She will ask a student to start by counting one stride away, then two strides away, then three strides, four, and all the way up to ten strides away from the jump. She feels that teaching them to count in ascending order makes the rider continue to the jump, whereas asking them to count in descending order makes them back up to create the answer.

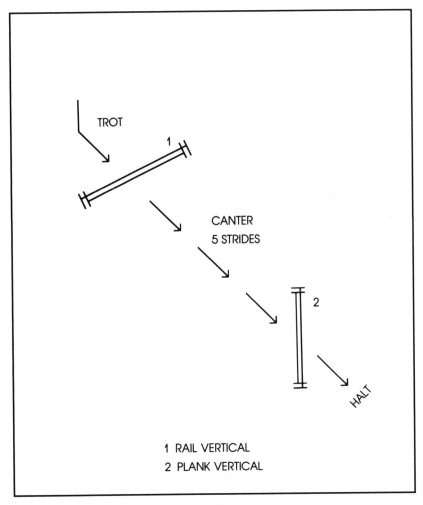

Counting Exercise

The first rider through gets six strides. "Most people do too much," she tells me. To the rider she advises, "Do just enough, not too much." Some of the riders forget to do the halt, some interfere with the horse's stride and several get a poor halt. The junior rider is a prime example of the latter as she lands on her hands after a crest release and has no time to effectively halt. "When you put your hands on his neck, he just falls on his nose more. Pick your hands up, bend your elbows, and use your back to get the halt."

They are all sent through the exercise again. "If you want to be

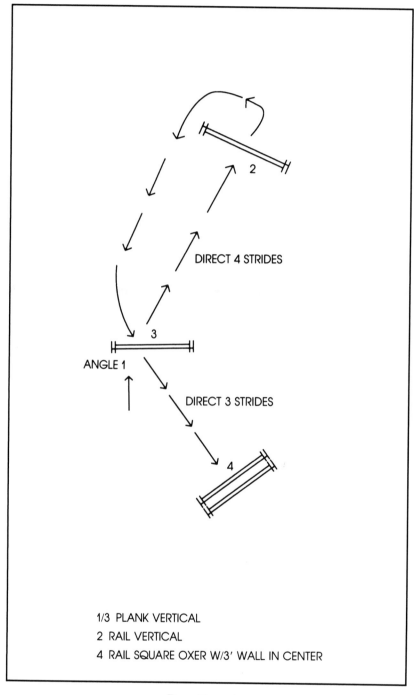

2

DIRECT 4 STRIDES

3

ANGLE 1

DIRECT 3 STRIDES

4

1/3 PLANK VERTICAL
2 RAIL VERTICAL
4 RAIL SQUARE OXER W/3' WALL IN CENTER

Pace Exercise

perfect, just be perfect. Just do it. Count aloud, stop on a straight line. Do that every time. Think like that."

They are given a new exercise where they jump on the angle at the first jump to make a straight line to the second. They are to get four strides in this line. After that, they are to roll back on the first fence backward and ride three strides directly to an oxer. "Ride it in a nice hunter rhythm. As smooth as you can do it. You want the same pace or rate of speed in the turn that you need between the jumps, so you don't have to speed up or slow down between the jumps."

One horse has trouble with his lead changes in the course and Anne sends the rider off to work at the walk on leg yields to remind the horse about leg without getting him flustered. The rider will work on this issue until her next turn at the jumps. Anne notes that all riders are training all the time. They may train the wrong thing, but they are always training. Therefore, it is important that they be consistent and firm in their demands without losing their tempers or clashing their aids.

Once everyone completes the exercise, fulfilling all the demands of the course and the instructor, a new exercise is introduced. The riders are asked to trot the spooky yellow and black boxes and circle around at the canter to the swedish oxer liverpool jump. "The biggest thing about a spooky jump is holding your line and sitting down in front of it. Jump the jump and don't be wimpy. Hold your line. Sit right down and cluck, getting them right over it."

One rider has trouble with the turn as she allows the horse to pull her down on the neck. A big, strong horse, he roots in the bridle and she has learned to try to make turns by resting one hand on the neck while pulling with the other. "If you keep hanging on his mouth, he'll never turn, he's much stronger than you are. You have to give and take . . . give a little bit. You have to feel the mouth. You have to have feeling. It's like in a car. If you ride the brakes all the time, the brakes run out. You need to train the turns, remembering horses are much stronger than we are. It's changing the pressure that gets them light. When he's nice, you be nice. If you just hang, he'll hang back in the turn."

Later, Anne works with an advanced student. They are working on the horse, making him a better athlete at the jumps. They work on getting the horse to gallop in a round shape, and as they achieve shape,

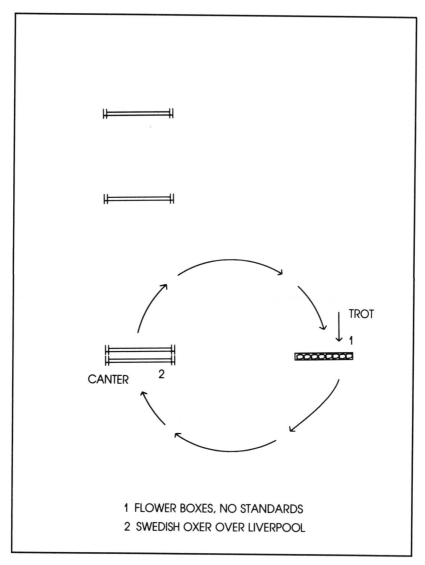

Introducing the Liverpool Jump

allow him to gallop to a jump. The rider tries to influence the takeoff
spot. "Don't protect him off the base . . . let him learn the deep distance," Anne counsels. They work on galloping a pole on the ground,
keeping shape. "Move the bit if his head comes up. When you stop
riding, you lose the jump." The rider repeats the ground pole several
times to learn the feel she wants over the larger jumps. "You should
have the same feeling in front of the jump as if it was just that pole on

the ground. Somehow you are telling him to change his structure. You, as a rider, have to figure that out. You need to be able to keep shape and gallop too." As they continue to work out feel, Anne tells the student to visualize success. "This is a mental sport. Feel it clean, picture it being jumped clean. Use the untapped resources of the brain." After

Kym Ketcham

Student Sandy Van Dyke

a few minutes they are successful in getting the rider to relax and duplicate the feel she had at the tiny jump over the larger effort.

Riding is indeed more than a physical sport. No one would mount you on a hopeless horse and expect victory. Given that your horse can do the job you desire, what separates the winners from the losers is knowledge and confidence. To win you must be psychologically tough and physically supple. You must be able to read your horse and influence him.

❑ *Clinic information can be obtained by contacting Market Street, Inc., P.O. Box 2366, Flemington, NJ 08822; 908-806-3669.*

FRANK MADDEN

"It's like learning to play the piano. You learn your notes and you learn tempo before you go on to play the more complicated pieces."

Kym Ketcham

FRANK MADDEN, IN PARTNERSHIP WITH BILL COONEY, PUT BEACON HILL RIDERS AT THE TOP OF THE JUNIOR RANKS FOR MANY YEARS. TOGETHER, THEY TRAINED SEVERAL MEDAL/MACLAY/USET WINNERS: STACIA KLEIN, CANDICE SCHLOM, JENNO TOPPING, MIA WOOD, AND CRAIG SCHEGOG. AN AHSA JUDGE WHO RUNS JUDGE'S CLINICS FOR THE ASSOCIATION, FRANK IS IN DEMAND NOT ONLY AS A TEACHER BUT ALSO AS A JUDGE AND CLINICIAN. IN ADDITION TO ALL HIS ACTIVITIES STATESIDE, FRANK IS INVOLVED WITH TEACHING IN SOUTH AMERICA, WHERE HE RUNS A REGULAR CLINIC PROGRAM AND IS DEVELOPING A HUNTER FUTURITY PROGRAM IN BRAZIL.

The Flat

Frank's teaching plan is to develop well-educated, well-rounded riders who are able to think for themselves. He wants to make people, not just riders, and that means more than teaching the basics of riding. And equally important, he teaches the riders how to handle the pressures that come with the competitive life. The rider for this lesson is warming up as we talk, and Frank says his more advanced students are encouraged to do that. "To me, that is the whole job of a teacher. If after a couple of years of training a student is not independent, someone hasn't done their job." Also, he points out that letting the rider warm up without direction gives the rider time to evaluate the horse's mood and abilities that day. "That's part of the warmup, to realize how the horse feels and how he will school from the way he feels."

Frank asks many questions of his riders, the Socratic method of teaching. He starts this lesson with a question, "What kind of frame do you like when you are loosening up?" Student and teacher agree on a long, stretching warmup. Once the horse has had sufficient time to loosen up, they begin to ask for more. "Just spend a second in the walk and change his frame into an attitude of listening to your aids. A little more collected, putting him at or on your aids. When you think about this, think about it beginning from back to front. Making sure the contact you are maintaining won't discourage him from going forward." Frank asks the rider what would prevent the horse from going forward. They agree that contact should be steady but not stiff so the horse won't have to defend himself from pressure on his mouth.

Frank asks questions to help the riders understand what they are doing. "I don't want them doing things to appease me or to appease their parents. I want them to really understand the nature of the horse and the nature of themselves. I'm always looking for feedback to see where they are coming from."

Working at a posting trot, the student is asked to show an extension of the trot on both short ends of the ring. So, we not only move him from the back to the front, but also forward and outward." The horse is slow to answer her legs and they work on a short gallop to get his attention. "It has to be a reflex on his part to answer your legs." Frank has her gallop on both ends of the ring to wake him up. "When you're teaching your horse a lesson to the aids, it doesn't have to be to the ideal degree. It's more important that the point is being made." Frank has her add some inside bend at the ends of the ring. "That will give him a little better understanding at the extension to go forward and where?" The rider responds correctly, "Go forward and outward."

The rider is asked to show a big circle with tempo. "Let your project on the circle to be having him accept the inside rein more and more, so you feel more and more of his weight so he can go from the inside to the outside rein."

The exercise is repeated in the other direction with a goal of getting the horse light to the right rein and leg. "The objective is to get him to move forward and outward." Frank reminds her to remain elastic through her arms. As she works on her objective, Frank tells me that it is important to teach the riders "That they are able to influence a horse with the aids or be able not to influence the horse. To know how to use the aids and how not to use them and knowing when to use them. The goal is to get the horse to react to the aids promptly but in a relaxed manner."

At the walk, the student is asked to show a shoulder-in at that gait. The horse is slow to respond and Frank suggests she use the spur to correct his dullness. "When you feel that stickiness to your leg and you're going to use your spurs to teach him about leg, use quicker and sharper pricks with your spurs to get a reaction. You can get him dead to spurs just as you can get him dead to legs by not doing something active when you are unhappy with the reaction you got." The rider is asked to straighten out and show the shoulder-out. Again, she meets some resistance. "When he does something wrong and you don't correct it—you are telling him what? That it's right, that it's okay. If you have the wrong kind of spur on or you are not using your spur right, you are not teaching him about legs."

The rider goes to the sitting trot without stirrups. She is told to maintain the tempo of the sitting trot while showing shoulders-in and shoulders-out. "Every now and then make a little check on where you are sitting. I want to see you just behind the vertical." The student is instructed to make sure that before and after lateral work, she gives the horse some time to straighten and go forward. The exercise is done in the other direction. They work on "self carriage," that is, getting the horse to carry the frame without a great deal of input from the rider. Frank asks the student why the lateral work is followed by some sort of extended work. "Yes, to make sure he is in front of you. The foundation of good riding is built on impulsion."

Coming down the quarter line, the rider is asked to perform a leg yield, keeping the tempo of the trot the same, not letting it decrease as the horse is asked for the lateral move. Following the lateral moves, the horse is asked for the canter before repeating the leg yielding exercise. "It's an important but basic concept about leg that when you use leg, the horse should move first forward from leg and then sideways." Frank tells me that simple exercises are the bulk of his flat lessons. He's not looking for glitz in the flat work but for the rider to get an understanding of how to put the horse in front of a rider's legs and how to keep him there—maintaining rhythm, changing tempo and adding those critical, basic elements in the simplest of lateral work. "From there you are building a platform for more sophisticated flat work. I don't see nearly enough of this attention to basics. It's like learning to play the piano. You learn your notes and learn tempo before you go on to play complicated pieces."

The rider continues to work her way through the exercise in both directions as Frank watches, explaining that the reason his students do all this basic work is so "In the end they don't have to ride. They are able to get enough quality moments in their riding to sense the moments of freedom, when they can allow the horse to carry himself. There are moments to ride and moments not to ride."

Both horse and rider are given a stretch break at the hand gallop before being asked to change direction holding the counter canter. "Hopefully, with the work you give the riders you are developing people. What I mean by that is that you are giving them lots of different personalities on the horse. There are just way too many problems in training a horse and executing a course to be able to do it with one personality. They have to be able to be strong at moments, be soft at others. It's a little bit like Dr. Jekyll and Mr. Hyde; they have to be able to be a monster one second and Cinderella the next. They have to be able to turn that off and on in a stride. There could be a place on course where the only thing that gets them through a combination or over a spooky jump is nothing more than guts and sheer willpower. The very next jump might be like a chess move; a very calculated, steady ride. If the rider isn't rehearsed in those different attitudes and personalities, the rider will be dissatisfied with the results."

Frank warns against doing the same thing over and over. "There is no way that riding around the outside of the ring is going to make you a tiger. On the other hand, if all you ever do is ride the hard ones, you'll never be a Cinderella." Frank says that he finds himself being more and more a manager of the riders' careers, rather than solely a trainer. "Managing situations, making sure the student gets a chance to ride this kind of horse over this kind of course, or that they get to the right kind of shows, or that they ride a hard horse, a green horse or that they get to go to Brazil with me to demonstrate. I am managing their educations." We then talked about the accusation that too many of today's junior riders are being called technicians rather than riders.

"I agree it's a big problem, but I don't think it's just a teaching problem—it's also the system. The top trainers and the AHSA have recognized the problem but perpetuate dullness by recognizing more and more horse show dates. What I teach at home to make better riders isn't backed up at the horse shows until finals time. No one wants to face the problems all year long, then the finals come along and everyone is suddenly interested in riding."

Jumping

"I like the jumps and the exercises of the jumps to do a lot of the teaching. Very often they are stronger than words for getting the point across. The horse and the course will produce problems for the rider to solve or prevent."

Our rider has shortened her stirrups in preparation. She is told to trot a small vertical on the diagonal and canter a larger vertical on the opposite diagonal. "I want you to do the two jumps three times each. I'd like to see you do them three different ways, showing different seats, different leads, different distances." Turning to me, Frank says he encourages mistakes in lessons. "I think it is so important that they learn it's not the end of the world when they make a mistake. They have to learn courage. It makes them understand how to prevent mistakes and correct them. I don't do anything to inhibit them from making mistakes." Frank mentions the importance of varying the lesson routine daily to prevent the riders and the teacher from getting in a rut.

Generally, Frank wants his students to school the horses in less equipment than they show in. A lesser bit, no martingale, no draws reins. He is not rigid on this point, however, believing that a rider should be familiar with the reaction the hrose gives in show tack. If the horse goes in a twisted bit at shows and never does so at home, the rider could be tricked at the change in the horse's reaction.

The demonstrator is asked to jump an end fence to teach her about quick, accurate riding. "When you don't have a lot of time to correct things—like a cut in, a bulge, whatever—you must be in your saddle in a position of leverage." He asks the rider to canter down the long side of the ring in a two-point position, finding her seat at the short turn before the jump. He also asks her to figure out which side (lead) causes which problem, so the rider "doesn't just relate to the mechanics of the exercise, but to the horse." He trusts the rider will learn how

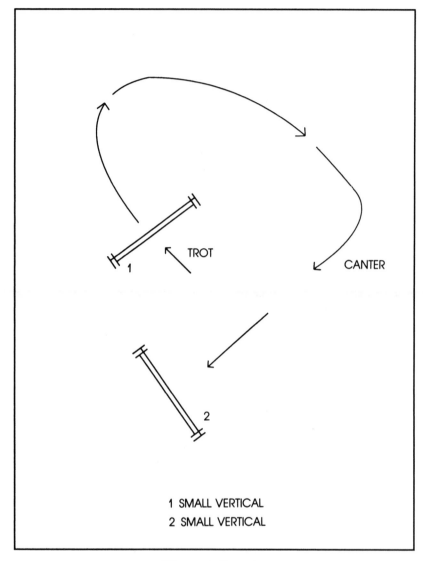

TROT

CANTER

1 SMALL VERTICAL
2 SMALL VERTICAL

Warmup Exercise

to relate this exercise to the ring when a similar problem appears. He wants her to remember the feeling of connecting and correcting.

The rider adds a long approach to a single jump on an angle after the end jump to help her measure pace and keep her track. "As far as position goes, I just work on the maintenance of it, it's bacially there." Frank admits his European and South American experiences have changed his opinion on the teaching of position. With riders overseas

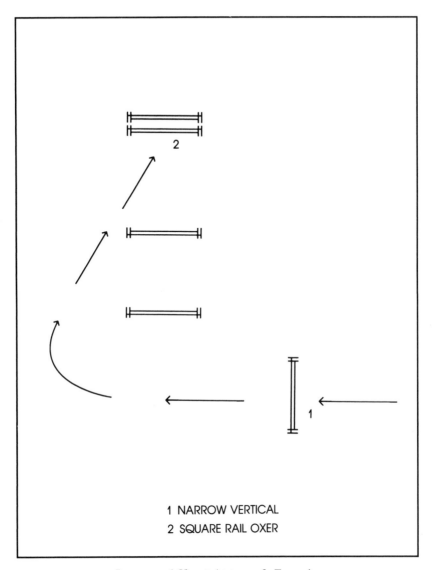

Long and Short Approach Exercise

"you obviously have a communication problem, yet you want them to learn something. You find you rely more and more on how you set up the jumps. What's amazing to me is how well people ride without instruction. I see more messed-up positions through poor teaching. In South America, I'll give a clinic and plant some seeds with the people I teach three or four times a year. I'll come back and see improvement. They learn to trust themselves and I see more growth with these kids

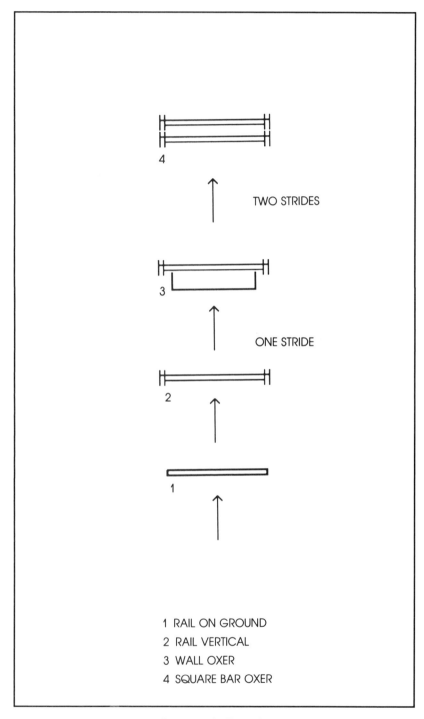

Gymnastic Exercise

who don't have a teacher to depend on for every move. Instruction is important but it shouldn't be too much."

I asked Frank to outline the composition of his average lesson. "My average lesson incorporates some independent work, some collected work, some extended work, a little gymnastic work and some steering work—at least touching on those bases every lesson." Good trainers, he tells me, move the jumps often with the goal of having the jumps manipulate the situation. "I think our riders jump way too many small jumps these days and that lets them get away with murder. In Brazil and Europe the smallest course the juniors can jump is three feet six inches, and it goes up from there. Because of their showing systems, the riders' positions are becoming more functional and correct."

Our student is going through a gymnastic as we talk. She has to trot in over a cavalletti and jump out through a triple consisting of a vertical, one stride to a wall and two more strides to an oxer. Frank quizzes her: "Where would you say you have to lengthen first? Where is your first shortening?" The rider figures out where she must go forward and where she must compress. Frank raises and spreads the fences, noting how the distances ride will now be different. "The gymnastic is not an entity in itself, but a dissection of problems," Frank tells me. He finds it a good place to discover horse and rider weaknesses. The junior says she finds the exercise harder to do well off one lead than the other. They work on the more difficult lead, sorting out the problems of horse response.

The next exercise is a line that backs up the problems found through the work in the gymnastic, incorporating the long and short distances, adding a steering subtlety to the swedish oxer. The rider is asked to reverse her direction through the jumps and reminded to steady early enough in the four strides so that she doesn't stall out over the oxer, which would make the long three harder. She over rides the final three, taking a rail down. Frank wants her to relate this to a show ride. "When you over ride a distance, the horse gets what?" The rider says her over ride caused her horse to get flat, taking the rail down.

The fences are raised again and a course given to the rider that allows for a few options, so that the rider can discipline herself to find the track needed for the required strides. "The important thing about striding in broken lines is to consider pace and line," Frank warns.

There are three bending lines on the course, and Frank wants to see the rider work out the track that will yield the lesser strides. "I

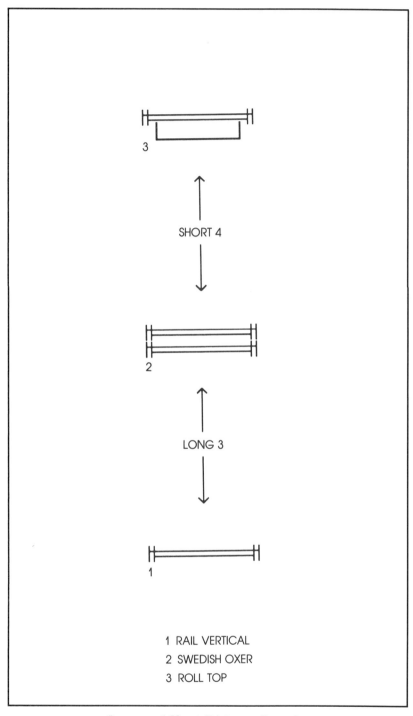

3

SHORT 4

2

LONG 3

1

1 RAIL VERTICAL
2 SWEDISH OXER
3 ROLL TOP

Long and Short Distance Exercise

want you to try and make it work the very first time. That's important, but if the first time through doesn't work to your satisfaction, get it again." The student works her way through the exercise with a couple of surprises. The horse isn't perfect in the exercise, but she works out the problems, getting the job done. The student and Frank discuss the lesson at its conclusion, pinpointing the mood of the horse that day and how it affected her ride. Frank wants his riders to have flashbacks to lessons when they encounter difficult days in the ring, flashbacks that will have them instantly react and correct from having been there before.

"What color should you have to that jump?" is a question Frank asks many of his riders. "Color" describes how the rider must change personalities to meet differing situations and various horses. He firmly believes riders must not be just one face riding one plane. They must be able to be aggressive, passive, firm, giving, nitpicking, relaxed. In his effort to make educated riders from the very beginning, he asks riders to know about horses as athletes, as individuals, as more than machines. He teaches even the youngest student to know the animal, its physiology, its needs and its senses. He finds an encouraging trend toward more involvement with the horse from the junior riders of today. He reminds his riders to work on their weaknesses, saying, "The chain is only as strong as its weakest link. If you don't know enough about your business, don't be surprised if you are not meeting your goals."

Versatility is important to Frank. From asking the riders to show different personalities on the horse to the management of the riding experience, including international opportunities, Frank's goal is to make people who ride well rather than ring robots.

❏ *Clinic information can be obtained by contacting Beacon Hill Show Stables, 86 Montrose Road, Colt's Neck, NJ 07722; 908-409-0303.*

C H A P T E R · 1 2

JUDY RICHTER and ANDRE DIGNELLI

"The horse should never be sacrificed for the rider's goals."

Kym Ketcham

JUDY RICHTER'S THIRTY YEARS IN THE BUSINESS HAVE LEFT HER WITH A RÉSUMÉ TOO VAST FOR THIS BOOK. SHE HAS BEEN INVOLVED IN ALL PHASES OF THE BUSINESS FROM TRAINING, TO CHAIRING AN AHSA COMMITTEE, TO JUDGING, TO RUNNING HORSE SHOWS, TO WRITING AND, OF COURSE, TO RUNNING HER OWN VERY SUCCESSFUL BUSINESS: COKER FARM. IT HAS BEEN A BUSINESS THAT LIKES TO OUTGROW ITS BOUNDARIES.

OVER THE YEARS SHE HAS TRAINED A WEALTH OF TALENTED RIDERS, INCLUDING SUSAN (BAUER) PICKNEY, ELLEN RAIDT, SCOTT NEDERLANDER, ALEX DUNAIF, LYDIA AND AMY THEURKAUF, ANDRE DIGNELLI AND PETER LUTZ. THE MOST RECENT, PETER LUTZ, WON BOTH THE USET AND ASPCA MACLAY FINALS IN 1991.

FORMER STUDENT ANDRE DIGNELLI STAYED ON WITH JUDY AT THE CONCLUSION OF HIS JUNIOR YEARS. HE WON THE USET FINALS IN 1985 AND THE USET TALENT DERBY IN 1987. SINCE THEN HE HAS COMPETED IN EUROPE AND BEEN A BRONZE MEDAL WINNER ON THE NATION'S PAN AMERICAN TEAM IN 1991. THAT WAS THE SAME YEAR HE PILOTED TURNING POINT TO THE GRAND HUNTER CHAMPIONSHIP AT THE NATIONAL HORSE SHOW. CURRENTLY, ANDRE IS TEAMED WITH THE JUMPER GAELIC, WINNING AND PLACING IN MANY GRAND PRIX CLASSES.

The Flat

The rider for this lesson is a professional from Alaska. She comes to the lower Forty-eight to learn as much as possible both for her own riding and to take back to her junior students. Judy has her begin with a loose, ordinary trot to warm up. "I think it's important when you are teaching that you have some kind of a plan of what you will cover in a lesson. That doesn't mean I won't change or modify the plan if it's going well, or if it's going badly."

With junior competition so demanding today, Judy says, "It's important for junior riders that their horses be rideable and obedient. We'll be working on that rideability today."

Judy believes it is very important at home to set up the ring like a Montessori classroom. "We always have some cavalletti out, some puppy jumps; things a rider can work on his own." She likes the Montessori approach because it helps students think for themselves and teaches them to solve problems without endangering themselves or their animals. However, Judy cautions, "I wouldn't want to see a student take on jumps of any size or lines of any difficulty by themselves."

The rider is told to add some cavalletti on the ground to her flat work. Two rails are laid out about twenty feet apart. They are placed across the center of our work area off a blind turn. She is asked to trot the poles in a figure eight. As the rider comes around a jump to find an approach to the poles, Judy tells her to use her eye early. "Look over . . . don't wait to get around that jump to look for the poles." Judy explains that she likes to put a lot of information into her lessons, much of which reinforces the basics, such as this cavalletti exercise, which by its placement teaches the importance of eye in riding. "In indoor rings especially," Judy says, "you have to look before you get around the jumps. The rings are usually small and crammed with fences."

"Kick him up in the bridle a little more, getting him a little brighter. You can ask him to bend a little around your inside leg or your outside

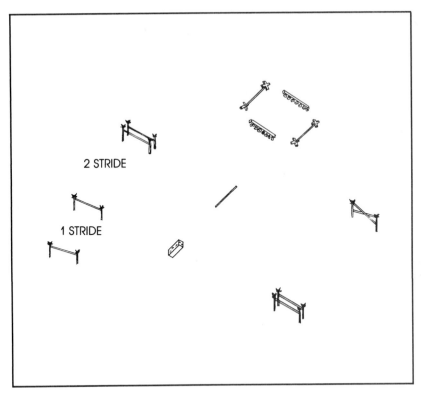

2 STRIDE

1 STRIDE

Rendition of the Montessori ring at Coker Farm

leg . . . limber up his neck." Judy is not advocating excessive head wagging. She wants the rider to be softening the horse by using both reins and both legs to bend the horse first one direction and then the other.

"Go to the sitting trot, to a shoulder-in, keeping it lively . . . lively . . . and then back to your ordinary trot for the rails." The rider is incorporating the bending exercises into the figure eight over the rails on the ground. "Do the same thing going the opposite direction, showing me the shoulder-in." Judy says it is important to work both sides of the horse and says "A rider should work in the horse's good direction first and the bad direction twice as long," constantly changing direction to keep the horse attentive and supple.

"Now a strong trot, sending him forward." Judy explains that she is working on the rideability of the horse. "He needs to be obedient both longitudinally and laterally." The rider alternates between shortening the stride, keeping impulsion, and lengthening the stride after the rail. Judy asks the rider to incorporate bending in both directions while working the figure eight over the rails. Including the rails ensures that the rider will keep reinforcing her eye and, consequently, her steering while she is learning to feel the horse's strides. Further, the use of the poles ensures that neither the horse nor rider will lose interest in his work.

"Canter. A lively, ordinary canter and then shorten and fit two strides between the poles. Look in. Give yourself some room. Lengthen after the rails and then shorten again for the two strides. Flying change, when you change direction. Make sure you get him together for the changes." Next, the student is asked to gallop, putting one stride betwen the poles. "Circle and put him together now. Then lengthen his stride and get the one [stride]." This is repeated so it is done well off both leads. Judy wants her rider to be aware that horses are different in each direction and directs her rider to "see that his stride is the same in both directions."

"Now you are going to add the stride again, keeping him lively and together. The student is told to lengthen after the pole before collecting her horse again to jump the poles in a short two strides. It takes her very little time to collect him back for the added stride. Judy gives the horse a break, saying that we sometimes forget horses are not machines and get overzealous with our training. The wellbeing of the horse is the trainer's responsibility, she tells me. "The horse should never be sacrificed for the rider's goals."

Another canter exercise that Judy finds useful is the counter canter. She asks our rider to demonstrate. "Counter canter around us, lengthening and shortening in the counter canter." Balance and obedience come from the counter canter work. The rider is directed to show her horse is obedient. "Make a right turn around the vertical and make a flying change to the counter lead to a circle on the new counter lead. Push his hindquarters out to keep it."

Judy asks the rider to demonstrate one more canter exercise she includes regularly in her lessons. "We'll start with his better direction first [to the right], and I want you to circle around me bringing him in and out on the circle." This is an exercise to make the rider aware of using both reins and both legs. She has the rider start in a medium circle and then look in. "Bring him in with both reins and both legs— look at me—bring him in. You'll find you need a lot more leg. Then go out again, keeping your leg. Once you're out there, be careful not to bend him any more than the arc of the circle." They repeat the spiral in and out as the rider discovers just how much hand and leg it takes to keep her horse forward in a small circle. The exercise is repeated in the other direction before the horse is allowed to walk.

This is an exercise that teaches the rider to keep to the track while keeping control of the horse's shoulders and haunches. "The two lateral evasions of the horse are to either fall in or fall out, so it [the spiral] is a good way to teach riders to use both hands and legs. It teaches the riders, too, how much leg they have to use to make small turns, while also teaching the horses how to make the short turns needed for the equitation tests and the jump-offs."

Jumping

A line of three jumps is set up for the rider. The distances ride easy between the first two jumps and long between the second two obstacles. As a warmup, the rider is first asked to ride the oxer alone on an angle and then angle the center vertical singly.

Judy has her just start out cantering the two small jumps to loosen up. Once the horse and rider are loose, the jumps are raised a couple of holes, to 3'3" or so, and the student is directed to gallop the oxer then collect in the turn before riding the vertical off a shortened stride. "Really fly the oxer, make a nice neat turn, balance, and jump the vertical slowly. Make the inside turn after the vertical, then fly back on the oxer." Riders and horses need to be comfortable at various speeds and with the various distances those speeds create. Judy works her students at all paces to ensure they will be.

The exercise is repeated to smooth out the rough spots. The rider is having trouble with the collected jump. "Really think about your line to the vertical. This time, keep your shoulders back, keep your hands still and remember to give. Try to get a little more to the base if you can." Judy recognizes that the rider is trying to force her eye to find a distance at the slower jump and urges her to let the pace reveal the distance. This exercise leads logically to the line with the forward three and the quiet three strides.

"This will ride nice and then ride long the first time," says Judy,

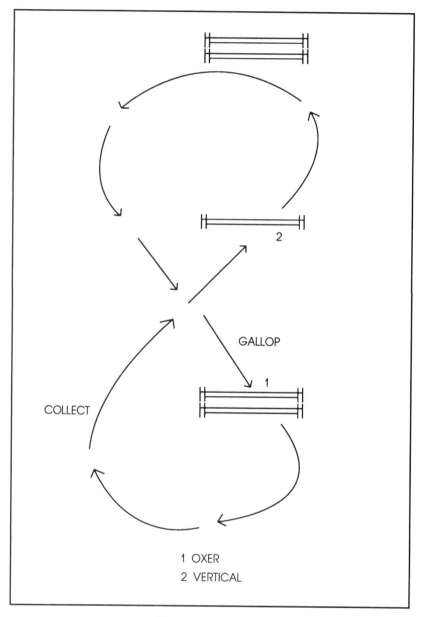

Warmup Exercise

pointing out the distances in the line. "Just canter up, do the three jumps, turn right and then come back. Make sure you organize him in the turn and come back with the continuing three first to the steady three." Judy watches, noting the rider rode the first part pretty well.

"If anything, she got there [to the second jump] slowing down and had to goose him a little for the second part. Then coming back she galloped for the jump and it was long. That made the tight part even tighter." It is explained to the rider that she needs to monitor her pace better; she is told to go forward to the first jump so she won't have to gun him for the longer part, and "Conversely, when you come back on it you should gallop up to it so the horse slows down for the jump, which will make the tight distance come easier." The oxers are raised. One of them is left a ramp that will function as an offset in one direction. Judy tells me, "You need to be careful with juniors and adults with the offset jumps. Keep them lower than the others."

There is more to this exercise than just getting the horse to expand and contract his stride. It is also an exercise about turning. "You'll see that if the horse slices part of the turn off, the jump will be a problem." At this point Andre advises the rider to take her time in the turns to get her horse balanced and calm. Then, he tells her, all she'll have to do is "free up and follow."

The exercise successfully completed, the horse is given a rest while the rider removes her irons.

"This is something we ask the juniors to do a lot. They ride often without their stirrups. We ask them to do their test work without stirrups too." The rider readies to repeat the exercise. "Don't forget your voice if you need the whoa . . ."

Because the rider is a little loose, the horse gets quick and almost gets two strides in the tight three-stride distance. While the rider walks, Judy asks her what she thought about her execution of the exercise. "That's another thing I like to do: ask them what they think, instead of just telling them all the time."

They agree it was not as smooth without irons as it was with them. Andre (who, according to Judy, sounds more like Judy than Judy does) points out that the rider's problems are with the turns. "Starting with the beginning of your lesson, you let the turns get rushed and ragged and now it's more important as the jumps have gotten bigger. If you had been very accurate from the beginning about keeping him out and keeping him light—only going forward when you told him to go for-ward—he would be more rideable right now."

Andre cautions the rider, "Don't let him use the turn to get his balance. Instead, get him balanced before you let him turn. You are using the turn to get his balance by pulling on him." Judy says the turn,

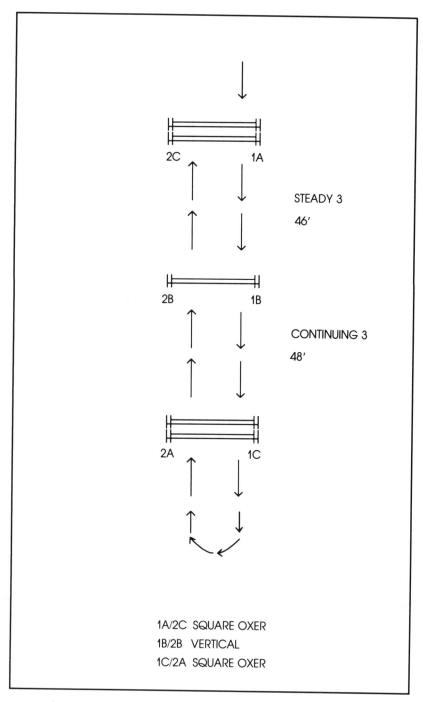

Rideability Exercise

James Leslie Parker

Student Peter Lutz winning the 1991 USET Finals, Gladstone, NJ

the track, the rhythm and the horse's balance all determine how the jumps will be. The rider is successful this time by slowing down her thoughts and taking care of the turns.

The physical part of the lesson is over. Judy talks with the student about problems they confronted. They talk about riding horses toward and away from the ingate and how it affects performance. They discuss how important it is for the horse to be rideable and responsive. This student critiques herself harshly, being much harder on herself than her teacher. "You have to be objective about what was good. When

153

you are on your own a lot, pretty soon everything seems bad to you, even when it isn't."

"Talent is nice but even the talented riders have to work hard to master the basics," stress Andre and Judy. The attributes they find in winners are intelligence and the willingness to work very hard. Those two features are vital for riding and showing competitively.

❏ *Clinic information for Judy Richter and Andre Dignelli can be obtained by contacting Coker Farm, Stone Hill Road, Bedford, NY 10506; 914-234-3954.*

C H A P T E R · 1 3

KIP ROSENTHAL

"Take control over the things you can control."

Kip Rosenthal

AS A JUNIOR RIDER, KIP ROSENTHAL WON THE AHSA HIGH SCORE CHAMPIONSHIP TITLES IN THE JUNIOR HUNTER AND JUNIOR JUMPER DIVISIONS. AS A JUDGE AND TRAINER, KIP HAS BECOME ONE OF THE POWER BROKERS IN OUR SPORT. SHE HAS JUDGED THE EQUITATION FINALS AND HER STUDENTS HAVE WON THEM. NOT ONLY DOES SHE OWN AND OPERATE THE HIGHLY RATED BENCHMARK FARM, TURNING OUT WINNING JUNIOR RIDERS AND CHAMPIONSHIP HORSES, BUT SHE ALSO WORKS AS A SPORTS PSYCHOLOGIST, HELPING ATHLETES FROM MANY SPORTS HANDLE THE PRESSURES OF COMPETITION.

The Flat

Kip Rosenthal is a rare combination. She holds a doctorate in clinical counseling psychology and has vast equine training credentials. By putting her two interests together she has developed a unique system of teaching that creates studious, confident riders. She treats her students with respect and humor regardless of their age or ability. Once she has taught her riders how to be students, she trusts them to learn by listening and observing. They learn to study problems and seek solutions.

"Take control over the things you can control and learn how to deal with the things you can't control," is one of Kip's sayings. In today's lesson, the riders will be challenged by the terrain to take control. Despite the steep hill they are working on, they must keep the horse in front of their legs, keep the horse "at" their hands and control the straightness (and balance) of the animal. Kip believes these are three things the riders should always be able to control.

Before the riders begin the lesson, Kip asks them questions about the challenges ahead. She has a dialogue with her students before and after each lesson. During the lesson itself, the students are not to think of what they might want to say. Kip teaches them to listen and listen with their whole minds. She says it is not possible for them to absorb information if they allow their brains to work on formulating speech. If the mind is busy with that task, it is blocked from receiving incoming messages.

Working on the side of a forty-degree hill, the riders will face some new problems of balance. Kip asks them to consider how the hill will affect the horses' balance and speed. They are quick to understand that the downhill section and the uphill section will cause opposite problems. They are asked to think about how their bodies can help keep the horses in balance regardless of the incline.

At the walk, the riders are given time just to feel the horses' balance underneath them. Because they are good students they pay attention to the effect the slope has on their horses' balance. Given time to absorb this, they move into the posting trot to discover the effect the hill has on evenness of pace.

Kip stands outside the circle being made by the students. "Most riders don't ride the outside of the horse. By standing outside, I can keep an eye on that." After giving the riders time to feel the hill, she asks them to add bend to their horses. "Don't overbend—that will cause stiffness and make the horse run through his outside shoulder. Ride both sides, bending the horse through his body at the girth."

"Halt. Now, which is worse? For your horse to take a step forward or a step backward at the halt?" The students correctly answer "backward" and Kip commends them, noting, "A backwards step is a horse falling behind the leg."

Returning to the trot, Kip reminds the riders when they bend, they should be able to feel the horse's "inside hind leg take a bigger step towards the outside rein." An increase in the trotting pace tests the riders' control of their mounts and control of their own bodies as the horses take larger steps. A serpentine up and down the hill adds control problems. "Feel your horse if he gets heavy, feel your horse if he gets behind, feel what happens if your horse falls in or out. It's not so important right now that you might not be able to fix what's not perfect, but be aware of what's happening. Don't get caught short. If your horses start to ramble on down the hill, think about using your weight to fix it."

Two of the riders have let their elbows get floppy. They are poking them out as they sit in the posting trot. "Your elbows out tell me you are primarily interested in riding the front of your horses, and that's wrong. When you keep your elbows bent by your side, you are able to work the full length of your horse." Kip isn't a big one for picking on rider position unless it is adversely affecting the horse's performance. "Horses teach people how to ride. It's been my experience that if you focus on position, I find you usually create a stiffness in that part."

Because the downhill tends to create a heavier horse in the hand, Kip sees that a couple of the riders are keeping that heaviness up the hill too, riding on the horses' mouths. "Relax a little up the hill with your arms and ride forward. Feel how much your horse will allow and accept. Make sure you get the horse in front of your legs but not by pushing with your seat."

Kip wants to see her riders making decisions themselves. She doesn't want them to rely on a big animal of limited intelligence for decisions of pace or direction. "Remember, your horses are amoebas; so why are you going to let them make decisions for you?" It is her way of teaching the riders to take control of what they can control. Her riders know that in Kip's world the horse comes first, and it is the rider's responsibility to make a happy horse who is also obedient.

The sitting trot is performed in a circle pattern on the side of the hill. "Down the hill, let your shoulders come back a little bit to raise up the front of the horse. Up the hill, stay with the motion of your horse. Not ahead of your horse. Ride in the center of your horse. There have to be times where you relax against their mouths."

Following a canter, Kip starts transition work. She tells me that when she asks riders to show transitions, she always sets specific places for their execution. The riders are asked to sit trot directly before Kip, pick up a canter when they are directly in front of a specific jump, and canter down the hill. At the base of the slope, they are to show a hand gallop up the hill, coming back to the sitting trot in front of Kip. They repeat this exercise until two things happen: first, that they show a real gallop, a sitting trot and a canter; and second, that they are precise with their timing on the transitions. It takes some time for the riders to be able to show a true gallop, and Kip notes that in a test situation they would not win if they are not able to show the differences in pace. "I've got to see the gallop, the canter, the trot."

A brief walk break precedes a request for the turn on the haunches. This too proves harder because of the hill. "Think of a leg-yield off the left leg. Slow him and leg-yield him." She reminds the riders they have the controls they need. "First you ask, then you tell, and then you demand."

One rider is putting more weight in one leg than in the other, and this is forcing her hip to swivel in the saddle. "Keep your weight even in your legs. Your hip is moving out to the side, and that will create problems for your horse. Stay centered on your horse."

Walk-canter transitions are next. The riders practice until they can keep the horses' shape when they ask for the canter depart. "Keep enough feel of their mouths so you don't lose your horses' balance or shape when you ask for the canter. If you feel your horses come above your hand, you have to add more pressure against their mouths. The moment you feel them accept your hands, relax and go with them a little—just allowing your arm to go with the horse, not going forward with your body." The riders are directed to try the transitions out on different places on the hill. "If you feel him getting strong, you are using too much hand and too much leg. You have to feel how little it takes to get it done. Not how much."

As the riders and horses rest, Kip explains that her students usually have a flat lesson once a week that may include some cavalletti. If they are to have a school over fences, they get a shorter warmup. The goal of the flat work is to create "circuits" the rider can open or close as needed. Kip points out to the riders that an average trip around a Medal/Maclay course takes a minute or a minute and a half. Of that time, maybe a half-minute at most is actually spent in the air. All the rest is flat work. To Kip, a push-button horse is one that responds correctly to the aids, ridden by a rider who has learned the responses he or she will get when the correct aids are used.

James Leslie Parker

Katie Brierly demonstrating ring concentration at Devon

Jumping

The first jumping exercise is over an in-and-out on a hill. The riders are to trot up the hill over the combination, fitting two strides in. They are to make a half-turn in reverse following the out and canter down the hill in one stride. It is a difficult exercise. The first rider fails to get the two strides. The second rider gets it, but the horse shifts to the right to fit it in. "I want him to fit the two strides in without shifting to do it. When you ride jumpers, if you can't control his straightness, and that is the high side of a swedish oxer, you've just had four faults. Sometimes you want to shift to make a distance work better, but you want to make the shift, you don't want the horse to shift on you."

Kip has not specifically told the riders how to shorten their horses' strides or how to slow them in the air. She is trusting that by watching each other go, they will figure out what to do in this situation. They get one chance at this exercise and then have to canter up the hill, getting one stride in the combination, make a half-turn in reverse and trot down the hill, fitting the two strides in. On fitting the two strides in, Kip advises, "I'd almost think to walk. On the jump in, I'd almost think to stop." The first horse to attempt the exercise gets one stride downhill. Again, Kip reminds the rider of her responsibility in this pairing. "When he left out the stride, what did you do with your body? Did you catch up with your body? Or did you haul off and land on him? If I ask my horse to wait and he leaves the ground, I won't get up and make it easy for him. I didn't ask him to leave. Don't accommodate your horse by flinging your body up his neck and making it comfortable for him when he jumps out from underneath you."

Proving that the riders are observant, the next rider doesn't follow her horse when he tries for the one-stride in the two. The remaining riders manage to get the exercise done by figuring out for themselves that they have to take back in the air and keep their hip angles open over the trot jump.

The next exercise consists of cantering the in-and-out in one stride uphill, making the reverse turn to trot down the hill, fitting two strides in the in-and-out. From there, they are to canter on a long approach to a swedish oxer before making a right turn back to a dry-ditch jump. "The ditch will back them off so you will ride up to it staying in the tack. Then if the horse falls back, you are in a position to do something about it."

A couple of problems present themselves during this exercise. One is the ditch jump and one is pace control. "As I said, the ditch is going to back them off. If you start by riding backwards to it and they back off, you're cooked. Ride a little forward, stay a little behind." One rider has a problem because when she asks her horse to go forward to the

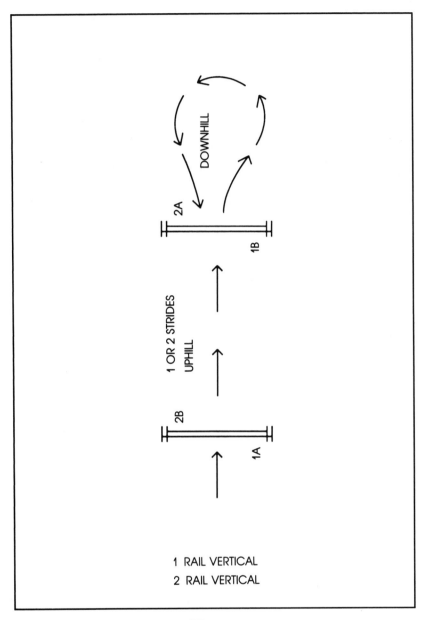

Warmup

ditch, she is pulling on the mouth as she pushes with her seat. Kip recommends that she ease up with her hands as she stays back.

Yet another rider finds the long approach to the swedish oxer to be ticklish. She is trying to find a distance and the hills are tricking

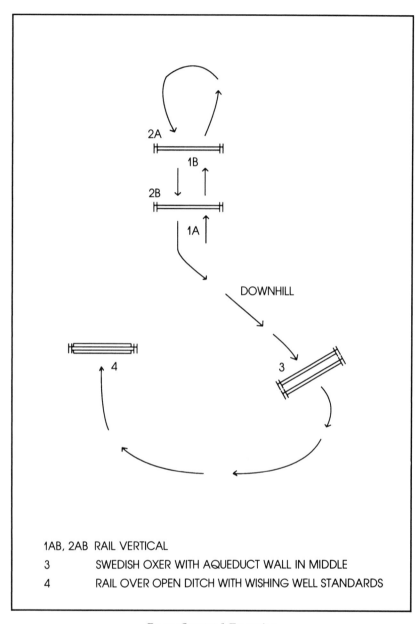

Pace Control Exercise

her eye. "Work out of the pace that you have. You are abandoning pace for jump, and that's wrong. Let the jump fit the pace. I'd rather have the jump change to fit the pace than have the pace change to fit the jump."

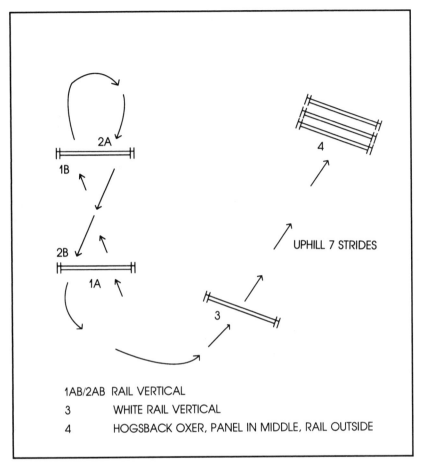

1AB/2AB RAIL VERTICAL
3   WHITE RAIL VERTICAL
4   HOGSBACK OXER, PANEL IN MIDDLE, RAIL OUTSIDE

Rider Control Exercise

The next test of rider control involves cantering up the hill to the in-and-out, making a right-handed turn in reverse so the riders can angle the combination to make room for a hard turn left back to a vertical on a steep grade and a continuing gallop up the hill in seven strides to a hogsback jump. This exercise reinforces the need for the riders to remember they must be giving and ride forward uphill if they are to get the strides. The left turn to the vertical is very tight and therefore fairly slow, so they will have to work out how to regain pace smoothly but promptly. "Pick up on the clues your horse gives you. Maybe you don't have to do so much, maybe you have to do more. Listen to your horse while doing as little as possible. Usually, less is better."

One horse gets rushed. He is bitted in a pelham, so Kip has the rider change her rein, placing the curb rein on top. That makes the curb rein dominant over the snaffle rein, and it is just enough extra leverage to convince the horse to come back. "With some horses you need to tell them with three degrees of pressure, with another, you might need thirty degrees. Figure out what your horse needs."

The final exercise is custom built for each of the riders' problems. All riders are to trot down the in-and-out in two strides, canter directly on to the ditch jump, make a left turn to the swedish oxer, follow a short bending approach to a white vertical, and canter up the hill to the hogsback. Two of the riders will trot the vertical and two will canter it. Besides the ditch in a new direction, which proves a problem for one horse, the other difficulty comes in the short bending approach to the vertical. The size and uphill nature of the swedish tends to take the riders past the vertical, making the turn difficult.

"Part of this exercise is very controlled. You have to show me patience and you have to show me riding forward." As the riders work through the problems of the course, Kip always tells them what they did right first before aiding them with the appropriate corrections they need for the parts they didn't get right.

"Never get ahead at a natural jump. Many times a horse will jump the natural jump the first time, but after they've studied it they get a little scared. If your horse stops, don't make it a process—use your stick. You have to want to get to the other side. Be careful when approaching natural jumps, not to allow yourself to get light in the saddle."

Concerning the problems the riders encounter from the aqueduct wall to the vertical, Kip advises the riders to find their line to the vertical when they are in the air over the oxer. "Look but take as much time as possible. Once you are on a line, you have time to work out the second jump. Staying in [on the line] allows you to slow up and shift if necessary." Kip tells me that finding the line early, even on a line as short as this one, gives the riders a place to get the horse back. This goes back to her flat work, where she required the riders to make transitions at specific points.

At the end of the lesson, Kip calls the riders in for a dialogue. She praises the riders who taught their horses to listen to them, saying, "When I'm on the ground, I'm your teacher. When you are on your horse, you are his teacher." She asks the riders if they have any ques-

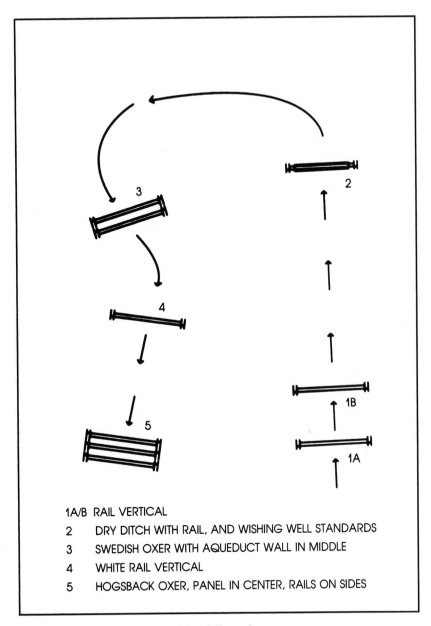

1A/B RAIL VERTICAL

2 DRY DITCH WITH RAIL, AND WISHING WELL STANDARDS

3 SWEDISH OXER WITH AQUEDUCT WALL IN MIDDLE

4 WHITE RAIL VERTICAL

5 HOGSBACK OXER, PANEL IN CENTER, RAILS ON SIDES

Final Exercise

tions about the lesson and what they learned. The responses are freely given, unself-consciously. They laugh about the difficulty of the terrain, one saying, "It's like your basics out here—it really tests your basics. If you can sit-trot out here, you can sit-trot any horse, anywhere!" One

Reflections of Killington

Emily Seidel keeping her eye to the track

at a time they say they learned the necessity on this course, of making the horse attend to their orders. They learned not to look for disappearing distances but to ride out of pace. They admit the need for a riding plan when combining terrain with natural obstacles and tough turns. One rider comments she finds the flat work on the hill to be harder than the jumping work. They agree that the field doesn't allow them to coast and that the topography forced them to be reactive.

Kip notes that this is a part of the learning process. Beginners, she says, have to be given a command, and then they have to think of each step in getting the horse to perform it. That means a slow response to the command. Intermediate riders progress to where they can recognize a command and go through their mental Rolodex to find the appropriate aids and implement them. The advanced student feels the

Alexis Densen in competition at Devon

William Meierfeld at the beginning of his career

problems, recognizes them instantly and is able to react instantly. She likes to tell her riders that they start with a small change purse into which they store their knowledge. As their experiences grow, so does the purse, until it becomes a huge bag of knowledge. After enough experience, they can pull from the bag all the answers they need. It is Kip's job to fill that bag until it becomes a steamer trunk.

While Kip works hard to teach her students about riding, she is also careful to teach horsemanship skills. She regularly schedules stable management "clinics" so students can learn grooming skills and learn about basic medicines, shoeing and more. The juniors are asked to muck stalls on some vacation days and are expected to clean their own tack. The total riding experience is what makes horsemen and horsewomen.

❏ *Clinic information can be obtained by contacting Benchmark Farm, 175 Ingleside Drive, Stamford, CT 06903; 203-968-1817.*

C H A P T E R · 1 4

CHRISTINA SCHLUSEMEYER

"Every rider can achieve a level of competence and success"

Kym Ketcham

CHRISTINA SCHLUSEMEYER'S QUIET HILL FARM IS SITUATED IN THE HORSE COUNTRY OF OCALA, FLORIDA. WITH THE HELP OF CO-TRAINER BOB BRASWELL, QUIET HILL STUDENTS ATTEND AS MANY AS FORTY "A" RATED SHOWS PER YEAR. TO DATE, THE FARM HAS TRAINED 65 NATIONAL CHAMPIONS. QUIET HILL STUDENT SCOTT HOFSTETTER WON THE MACLAY FINALS IN 1986. QUIET HILL TEAMMATE CHRISTY CONARD FOLLOWED SUIT TWO YEARS LATER. CHRISTINA'S DAUGHTER, HILLARY, IS WELL ON HER WAY TO A PROFESSIONAL CAREER; AT SEVEN YEARS OF AGE SHE WAS THE CHAMPION AND GRAND CHAMPION OF THE AHSA PONY FINALS. AND IT HAS BEEN ALL UPHILL SINCE THEN. QUIET HILL IS VERY PROUD TOO OF A RECORD THEY HOLD AT THE NATIONAL HORSE SHOW. THE FARM ENTRY OF SOFTWARE HAS WON THE AMATEUR-OWNER CHAMPIONSHIP A RECORD-BREAKING THREE CONSECUTIVE YEARS.

The Flat

Christina believes that riding should be available to the general public, not just to the wealthy. She believes that "Every rider can achieve his or her ultimate level of function and be confident at that level. The riders that I produce need to know that when they walk up to the ring it's between them, a series of jumps, the judge and their horse. They have to be independent and do it themselves. I want them very, very confident and able to reach a realistic goal. It may be adult amateur champion, perhaps qualifying for regionals, whatever. Give them a goal so that when they reach it, they have accomplished what they set out to do. Then you can reevaluate."

She also believes that this accessibility can be made available to hunter riders through careful purchasing. "My second goal is to make a hunter that costs less be able to jog in front of a horse that costs more. In the long haul, that makes the less expensive horse more valuable, which will help the owner pay for some of the tremendous expense of this sport. That makes riding more available to the general public. I like that."

The lesson begins with the rider working in a two-point, tracking left, which is her horse's stiffer side. Starting at the bottom and going up the rider's body from heel to head, Christina reminds the student of the interrelationship between all her body parts. She turns her attention to the horse to note, "The horse's mouth and head are the most important part of him because they are the most sensitive. But they are the parts you ride the least. You ride ninety percent of the horse with your legs, your weight, your body, your chirper, your artificial aids, your mental desire to go forward . . . all of that is what you do to ride. You are trying to make the motor of the horse [the two hind legs] come up underneath you and do the propelling, while you just control the front of the horse with not even ten percent of your riding ability."

"Your goal is always to be in the center of gravity. If your center of gravity is over his, he'll be comfortable and happy. A happy horse helps you out when you're doing a lousy job." Christina reminds us that riders of all levels make mistakes sometimes. "You could be a great, successful grand prix rider and be doing a lousy job jumping around your fourteenth Grand Prix. Say you left too long to a very wide oxer. A horse that trusts you to see to his comfort will help you out at those times."

Our student this day is one who lives over a thousand miles from Quiet Hill and therefore has to do much of her riding at home without the watchful eye of Christina. Knowing that, this lesson is a reinforcement of basics as well as homework for the rider to practice when she is on her own. Christina feels that students unable to afford a lot of lessons can make good progress with fewer if they practice the skills they learn at the lesson when they are on their own.

The rider's leg wants to draw up, becoming short, and it tends to slip ahead of her. Christina keeps her in the two-point. "When you are riding recreationally, do more two-point work. If you don't have a good leg position you won't have a good seat and you won't be solid enough to make your horse perform."

Hilary Schlusemeyer demonstrating a half-seat position

This rider is not graced with a long leg, but, her trainer notes, she needs to look as if she has length. "Check on yourself as you are riding around. How's my leg? Get into your two-point and stretch down into your heel. You'll only be comfortable by getting your leg into the correct position." Christina asks her to exaggerate the drop into her heel. "I want her to stretch her calf out like a piece of undercooked bacon and wrap the inside of it around this horse. I don't want to see the back of her boot, where it is stitched together, getting dirty. That would mean she was using the back of her calf rather than the inside." Christina likens the lower leg, from the knee to the ankle, as the computer keyboard used to relay direction and motivation to the horse.

"Keep your leg long, and go to the sitting trot. Don't let his stiffness at the sitting trot force you back into the short, propped leg, or you might as well chop your legs off for all the effect they have." Christina has the student change back and forth from two-point to three-point, teaching the rider's leg to stay long and deep in both seats.

"From the posting trot, let's extend the trot . . . use that lower leg, pushing the horse forward. Use that artificial aid for him [the spur] because he's dead-sided, but use the spur just to enforce your leg, not be a substitute for it. The next time you ask, you want him to respond to your leg, not the spur. Your artificial aids should make the horse respect your leg, not question it. Never use the spur or the stick as a lifeline. You have to be able to disassociate the artificial aids as soon as you can." She asks the student to extend the trot more: "Do it like you're trying to get the top call in the USET. Make your horse do what you want him to do, even if you have to sacrifice a little form to get it done. Form over function is fine, but the first and most important thing to do in any class you ride in is to make your horse function. If you have to give up some little niceties, give them up. You have to get the job done first. You won't make the jumpoff, the tests, the second rounds unless you succeed in the first round."

The rider is asked to slow down and go to the sitting trot, leaving her leg long. She is reminded to use a stick to help activate his haunches. "When you don't like his reaction to your leg, give him a tap with a stick." A reverse of direction takes him to his better side [the right], where the rider asks for another extension to the trot. "In a circle of this size he should be in a half-moon shape, with your leg in the exact middle of the shape. You want him to maintain this bend all the time. You should be able to glance down and see his right eye only. Don't

Kym Ketcham

The extended trot

do it by cramming his head in, do it by pushing his middle out with your inside leg to the soft, receiving outside leg, which will prevent him from drifting out on the circle." Christina notes that horses rarely move in circles. They travel in an elliptical, or oval, shape that takes them towards where they want to be: towards the outgate, towards a friend, towards the trailer, towards the pasture. Sometimes they'll make an ellipse away from where they don't want to be: away from the birds, the spooky jump, the loose dogs. "There is always something in his brain that is telling him where he would like to be and it's usually where he isn't. This means you have to be constantly changing everything, responding to his desires to be elsewhere."

"I need to have your ankle attached to the stomach of this horse as though you had Velcro there." Christina says that many beginners spend time pinching their knees into the saddle, and she has found the Velcro metaphor successful in getting young riders to learn the position, power and strength of lower leg.

The student is given a short walk break while her stirrups are taken away. "I think it's better to ride with no stirrups five minutes each day than to ride with no stirrups for a whole hour once a week. I think you get to the point where you are tired, and obviously you get to the

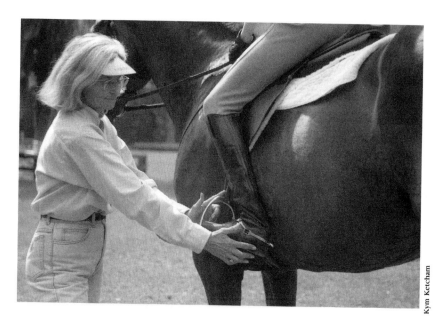

Kym Ketcham

Christina fixes the "Velcro leg."

point where it really bugs the horse; after all, there is just so much strength you have. The whole point of riding without stirrups is not to torture the horse, but to improve the strength of your lower leg, to work on your balance and work on using the lower leg."

The student is asked to post the trot and then to half-seat without stirrups. "This is something you should make yourself be able to do easily. Not for five minutes, but for forty-five seconds or so, until it looks easy and feels easy."

Christina asks the rider to pick up her stirrups, drop them, pick them up again. This is something she feels her riders need to practice so they can do it very quickly in the ring. She tells the rider to practice this at home to keep sharp, saying, "You never know when it might save a class for you."

With stirrups, the trot is extended and the horse is brought in to a small circle. "That was an ellipse. Do it better . . . keep him out . . . shorten your reins so your body doesn't twist in the circle." The horse is allowed to go out and reverse direction before coming back to a small circle in his stiffer direction. "If you ride with your reins too long, it will make your body twist and then you won't be over the center of gravity anymore. Shorten your rein length more often."

Another reverse into a small circle is performed by asking the horse to give to the inside leg and rein. Christina asks for a shoulder-in with an exaggerated bend because this horse tends to be stiff through his neck. That accomplished, the rider asks her horse for a long, low trot on a very loose rein, which allows him to stretch.

The canter work is next. In preparation, Christina moves the lesson to the side of a small hill, which she says works the horse's back end while teaching the rider balance and continuity of pace on the slope. She has her student begin at the trot, working on not allowing him to change pace as he goes up and down the hill. The student practices posting trots, extended trots, and slow sitting trots—the three gears of the trot. Christina sees that the rider is not keeping track of her rein length often enough. "Your hands need to remain in an invisible cigar box [about the size of a school pencil box] in front of the saddle. If you need to turn, shorten, lengthen, make a quick turn back in a jump-off, or need to make a rollback, you need to have your hands in the same place. To do that, and to effectively ride the horse, you need to lengthen and shorten your rein length lots more often than you are doing." Christina finds the box image most useful with young riders. They quickly learn not to "leave their box" to steer their ponies. Christina notes, "Lengthening your reins a lot is just as important as shortening your reins." She asks the demonstrator to show one place the lengthening is applicable. The rider is asked to halt. She executes the halt properly, with the slightest easing on the rein pressure when the horse gives in to her command. "The release after the halt is the passive reward that makes the horse happy he stopped when you asked." This gives her a chance to remind the student how horses learn, which is often by *not* asking them for something. "Just like a child who doesn't do homework...you bug him and bug him and bug him, and then when he does his homework you don't bug him...that's his reward."

As the rider begins her cantering up and down the hills, her leg draws up again. She is immediately put back into the two-point to get length before she is allowed to sit again. "On the downhill part, lighten your seat a little and let him balance bringing his legs up underneath him. On the uphill part, you want to give a little extra push and power so he keeps up his motor. I want his motor the same up and down the hills." A turn on the haunches at the walk is used to change direction before renewing the canter. It is a "checkup" to make sure the horse is listening to the rider's leg. Christina warns that a lot of practice on the turns on the forehand and haunches tends to aggravate horses, so she doesn't drill them on it. She also forgoes a lot of backing up work, not so much because it angers the horse, but rather because they learn to anticipate it and back up at every halt. "There is so much halt work in today's equitation tests without backing up, it seems counterproductive to practice it."

Jumping

The student is asked to warm up by trotting a crossrail back and forth. Christina is firm about teaching her students that "Jumping is flat work with obstacles in the way." She watches the rider work out the bending turns and straight lines to the warmup jumps. "When you're jumping, you want your vertebrae very soft and elastic, so that from the top of your neck to the base of your tailbone, you have all of your vertebrae nice and relaxed like an accordion. You want your back to lengthen and expand continuously at the sitting trot and canter and when you are closing over the jump. When you need your back to contract like an accordion being pushed in, you want to be able to do that very passively so your back stays elastic. People don't jump—the horse does the jumping, so basically the rider's job is to be in the position of least interference."

Christina wants her riders to understand their jobs. The job of not interfering, the job of letting the horse jump up to the rider, the job of controlling speed and track through flat work. She lists for me all the things a rider doesn't have to do when jumping: "A rider doesn't have to throw herself on the horse's neck, doesn't have to flap her elbows, doesn't have to round her back, doesn't have to stand up in the stirrups. All a rider has to do is tip her hip and wait for the horse to jump up."

She has the student drop her stirrups and canter the exercise in her two-point position. "Don't lean, let him jump up to you." She is allowed to pick up her stirrups but is now told to close her eyes when she finds the line to the jump. "Feel him crouch . . . that's when you tip your hip down and wait." Christina likes this exercise because the rider can't anticipate the jump but has to rely on feel. "You should feel as if a puppeteer is pulling on your hip strings, pulling your pelvis toward the last braid on the mane. That curls your hip down, makes your pelvis tilt so your bottom comes up, closing the angle between your body and your upper leg and leaving your back nice and flat."

A vertical is made and the exercise repeated. The rider is told to extend her approach to the jump and to close her eyes farther away. "When you feel him crouch...tip your hip." To add to the difficulty, the rider repeats the exercise without eyes and without irons. "If you can feel when the horse is going to jump and can tip at that time, it really helps your equitation, because then you aren't doing all the affectations that riders adopt."

The next exercise is a combination of vertical, vertical, oxer. It is a nice one-stride to a tighter one-stride. This is used to work on the rider's form without compromising the horse. "All I want to see with your body is tip one, tip two, tip three...that's all. You should look the same through this combination as you did over the little warmup jump. All you have to do in a gymnastic is find the first jump."

She warns the rider that the distances are going to get easier with repetition. "Once a horse knows what he's doing...from then to the point of exhaustion, the distance gets shorter, as long as he isn't over-

Kym Ketcham

Hilary Schlusemeyer demonstrates allowing
the horse to close the hip angle.

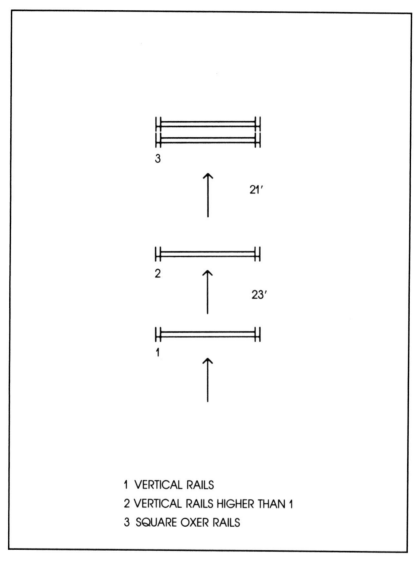

First Exercise

faced." The rider is told to come back through the combination without her stirrups. "Removing the stirrups for jumping highlights all the faults of a rider." Our rider goes through, rounding her back and ducking over the last two jumps. A discussion follows on what happened to her form without her stirrups. She is reminded to "concentrate on keeping your back flat and tipping your hip."

With each pass through the combination, the rider has found a different distance to the first jump; sometimes long and weak, sometimes tight, but always different. This is the result of her flat work on the circle and approach to the jump. "The important part of this is how you are riding the half-turn and the straight line. That part of this exercise is really between you and him. It has nothing to do with me, because if you do that badly, you are riding below your ability . . . and that drives me crazy. You are not making the best turn you can make! For as long as you ride courses, think of the course as being good flat work, correct flat work, with some canter steps over obstacles in the way. He jumps, you're flat. So you do your job and let him do his job."

The rider moves on to doing the exercise with her eyes closed. She is able to stay very still, so she is asked to come back with her eyes open and seek the same feel. She performs the exercise well and is asked to drop her stirrups.

The rider has had a chance to work on controlling her body over the jumps as well as sorting out her responsibilities toward the flat work, so she is moved on to a small course. "I want you to keep ninety percent of your mind on how you affect the horse on the flat in between these jumps."

The rider gets the job done, tentatively riding the unknown distances. She is encouraged to critique her own ride fairly. Now that she knows how the strides ride, she will be able to take more time mentally, to wind her way around the jumps. Christina reminds her that "When in the ring, it's just you, the jumps and the judge." One jump is added to the next course (fence 10). Our junior is reminded to ride up to the final oxer rather than waffle on the long approach. "Be on the kick there. If the opportunity presents itself to be brilliant, do it. Of all the things you can do, just do them better." Christina tells her student that every class in the show ring is graded on the curve, that is, in relationship to the others in the class. She might win one class with a mediocre trip or maybe place fifth with the trip of her life. "Be the best rider you can be and let the ribbons take care of themselves."

In this course, the rider has two problems. She parked to the first fence on the three-stride line because she knew the distance was tight. "You know what we call that? . . . Losing early. We want you to put off losing until later. Find what you find as a distance there and then cope with the tight three. Don't lose the class by missing the distance to the

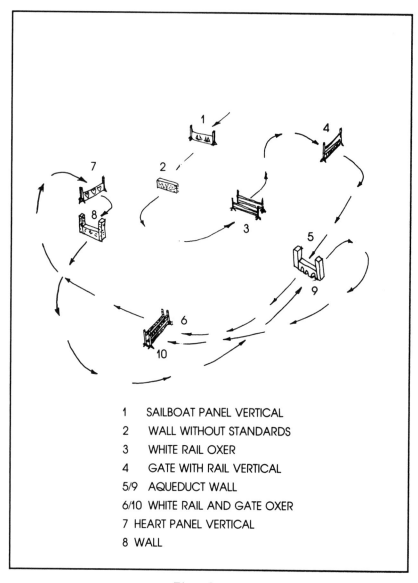

1   SAILBOAT PANEL VERTICAL
2   WALL WITHOUT STANDARDS
3   WHITE RAIL OXER
4   GATE WITH RAIL VERTICAL
5/9 AQUEDUCT WALL
6/10 WHITE RAIL AND GATE OXER
7 HEART PANEL VERTICAL
8 WALL

First Course

first jump in anticipation of trouble later. Don't lose before a problem presents itself... worry about the distance later." The other difficulty the rider had was the difficult first line. While it wasn't a major mistake it wasn't blue-ribbon material either. She repeats the first three jumps to work out the tough track from one to two to three so that it looks easy.

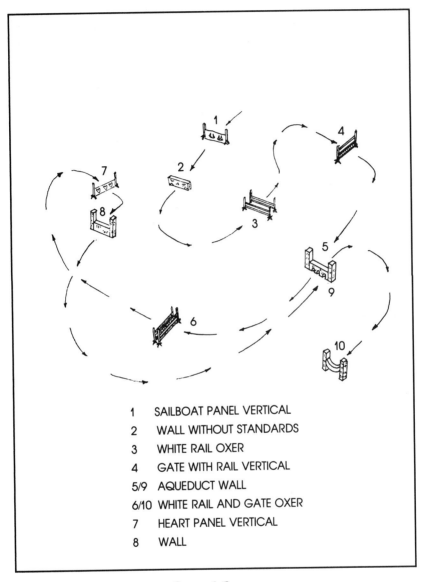

1   SAILBOAT PANEL VERTICAL
2   WALL WITHOUT STANDARDS
3   WHITE RAIL OXER
4   GATE WITH RAIL VERTICAL
5/9   AQUEDUCT WALL
6/10   WHITE RAIL AND GATE OXER
7   HEART PANEL VERTICAL
8   WALL

Second Course

From choosing attainable goals to riding preparation, Quiet Hill riders are able to fulfill their goals regardless of their abilities. It is a system that makes winners out of every rider from Maiden to Medal.

❑ *Clinic information can be obtained by contacting Quiet Hill Farm, P.O. Box 2586, Ocala, FL 32678; 904-629-4459.*

INDEX

Page numbers in *italics* indicate illustrations.